Water Politics in Northern Nevada

SECOND EDITION

T0303606

WILBUR S. SHEPPERSON SERIES IN NEVADA HISTORY

Leah J. Wilds

Water Politics in Northern Nevada

A CENTURY OF STRUGGLE

Second Edition

UNIVERSITY OF NEVADA PRESS
Reno & Las Vegas

WILBUR S. SHEPPERSON SERIES IN NEVADA HISTORY

Series Editor: Michael S. Green

University of Nevada Press, Reno, Nevada 89557 USA

www.unpress.nevada.edu

Copyright © 2014 by University of Nevada Press

All rights reserved

Manufactured in the United States of America

Design by Kathleen Szawiola

Library of Congress Cataloging-in-Publication Data

Wilds, Leah J.

Water politics in northern Nevada : a century of struggle /

Leah J. Wilds. — Second edition.

pages cm. — (Wilbur S. Shepperson series in Nevada history)

Includes bibliographical references and index.

ISBN 978-0-87417-951-4 (paperback : alkaline paper) —

ISBN 978-0-87417-952-1 (e-book)

1. Water-supply—Political aspects—Nevada—History. 2. Water resources development—Political aspects—Nevada—History. 3. Water reuse—Political aspects—Nevada—History. 4. Newlands Project (U.S.)—History. 5. Truckee River (Calif. and Nev.)—Environmental conditions. 6. Carson River (Nev.)—Environmental conditions. 7. Environmental policy—Nevada—History. 8. Nevada—Politics and government. 9. Social conflict—Nevada—History. 10.Nevada—Social conditions. I. Title.

TD224.N2W55 2014

333.91'6209793—dc23 2014020822

This book is dedicated to
the love of my life, Robert Dickens,
and to the light of my life,
Viki Wilds

Contents

Illustrations

Preface

This book is a political history of conflict over water resources in northwestern Nevada and an analysis of regional approaches to resolving those conflicts. The waters discussed are conveyed by the Truckee, Carson, and Walker River systems. The use, allocation, and ownership of these waters have long been the subject of legislation and litigation.

The first edition of *Water Politics in Northern Nevada,* published in 2010, dealt with water policy and legislation concerning the Truckee and Carson River water systems. This revised edition brings the reader up-to-date on the implementation of the 2008 Truckee River Operating Agreement (TROA), including ongoing efforts to preserve and enhance Pyramid Lake. The second edition now also includes a discussion of the Walker River Basin, following a major project undertaken to address concerns about the health and viability of Walker Lake. The approaches taken to save these two desert treasures are offered as models for resolving similar water resource conflicts in the West.

The audience for this book includes scholars and students interested in water politics, contemporary environmentalists, new residents to the West, and those interested in regional and local natural resource history. Every effort was made to make this book accessible and interesting to both an academic and a lay audience.

Many people contributed to the writing of this book. I would like to thank all of the individuals who made themselves available for interviews. I would like to thank Chester Buchanan for helping me better understand the role of US Fish and Wildlife in the water acquisitions process and David H. Levin for his excellent editorial skills. I am indebted to Donald B. Seney, emeritus professor of government at the University of California and consultant to the US Bureau of Reclamation, who gave me access to the wonderful oral history he collected about the Newlands Project. Support for the research and writing of the second part of this book came from the Walker Basin Project. I would like to thank all of those who were involved in that project, especially the scientists who conducted research in the Walker Basin. And finally I would like to give an especially warm thank-you to Senator Harry Reid, without whom none of what is detailed in this book could have been accomplished.

Water Politics in Northern Nevada

SECOND EDITION

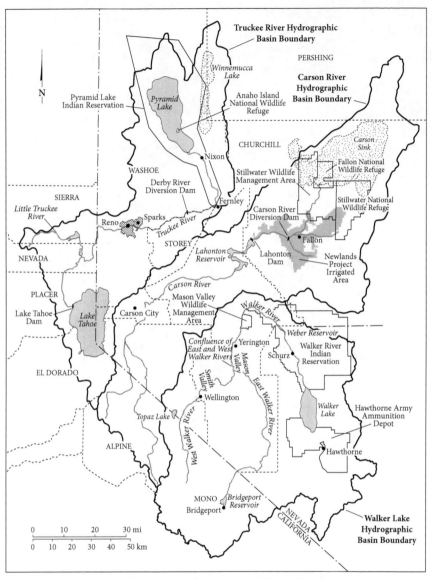

*Hydrodologic Features of the Carson and Truckee River Basins
and the Walker River Basin*

~~~~~~

Introduction

Contemporary conflict over the use of the waters of the Truckee and Carson Rivers was largely the result of the Newlands Project, the first reclamation project undertaken by the Bureau of Reclamation. Completed in 1915, the Newlands Project vision was simple: capture and store the combined waters of the Truckee and Carson Rivers to irrigate nearly a half-million acres of land, primarily in Washoe and Churchill Counties. Although the project never irrigated more than 73,000 acres, an average of 406,000 acre-feet (a-f) of water was diverted to project lands for decades.

The natural terminus of the Truckee River is Pyramid Lake, a desert terminus lake on the Pyramid Lake Paiute Reservation. The lake is home to the remains of a Lahontan cutthroat trout (LCT) population. It is also home to the unique and prehistoric cui-ui fish, which are found only in Pyramid Lake. These fish were declared threatened and endangered, respectively, under the Endangered Species Preservation Act of 1966. Not only did the decrease in flows over the years threaten the fish and their ability to spawn, but the decreased volume of water in the lake, combined with higher salinity levels, also threatened the lake's ability to support any aquatic life.

Beginning in the 1960s, the Pyramid Lake Tribe began to challenge the right of Newlands Project users to continue to consume that much water. Other users—environmental, urban, Native American—engaged in numerous legal battles over who had the right to use how much water from the Carson and Truckee Rivers and toward what ends. The fact that both rivers are shared by California and Nevada only exacerbated those conflicts.

Beginning in the 1980s, the federal government, itself involved in many of these lawsuits, encouraged the parties to enter negotiations to overcome their differences. Sponsored by Senator Harry Reid, the settlement that was reached was incorporated into Public Law (PL) 101-618, passed by Congress in 1990. Since that time, efforts have been made to implement its many provisions. One of those provisions required additional negotiations to create a new set of operating criteria for the Truckee River. The end result has been a much more flexible operating system for the river, enabling competing users to have most of their water needs met most of the time. That effort took more than seventeen years, ending with the signing of the Truckee River Operating Agreement on September 6, 2008. All of the provisions of PL 101-618 are not yet fully implemented. Until they are, the provisions of that law will not become "fully effective." Efforts are under way to make this happen.

The Walker River system presents, in some sense, a more complex water resource allocation and use situation. Unlike the Truckee and Carson, the Walker does not involve the federal presence of the US Bureau of Reclamation. Water storage and diversion infrastructure features were privately funded and constructed. Management is provided by a private irrigation district. The natural terminus of the Walker River is Walker Lake. As irrigated agriculture became a dominant aspect of the economy in the Walker Basin, more and more Walker River water was captured and stored in two reservoirs to be delivered to irrigated lands. By 1925 96,000 irrigated acres were in production in the Walker Basin. By the middle of the twentieth century, the lake level had dropped 145 feet. By 2007 it dropped another 4 feet. Resulting changes in water quality—due in large part to increased salinity levels—threatened the aquatic life dependent on the lake as well as the sustainability of the lake itself.

As was the case with the Truckee and Carson Rivers, increased competition over the use of Walker River water has resulted in decades of litigation between agricultural, Native American, and environmental interests. A 1993 court-ordered mediation to settle their differences out of court resulted in stalemate. The parties resumed litigation.

Concerned about the deterioration of Walker Lake, Reid helped secure passage of PL 109-103, the Energy and Water Development Appropriations Act, in 2005. Section 208 of that law directed seventy million dollars to the University of Nevada for what became the Walker Basin Project. The major policy goals of that legislation were to purchase water from willing sellers for delivery to Walker Lake and to do so in a manner that would improve the ecological health of the Walker River and enhance the local economy.

This, then, is the story of very different approaches to solving two sets of water policy conflicts in northwestern and central Nevada. It is the story of leaders and leadership. It is the story of scientists engaging in "civic" science. It is the story of conflict and cooperation. It is, at its heart, the story of people struggling to overcome a contentious past so that a precious resource—water—can be shared in ways that meet the needs of the future.

This work is important for a variety of reasons. It captures the processes and people who came together to resolve more than a hundred years of conflicts—conflicts that were complex enough to befuddle Congress and the courts throughout that time period. It is important because it describes the beginning of the end of an era in which agricultural interests dominated western water policy—and when agricultural uses of water were considered superior to urban, environmental, and Native American interests. More than four hundred million dollars in new federal appropriations have been distributed to help the West adjust to new water management regimes, improve infrastructure to save unique and endangered species, and achieve the socially and legally just recognition of Native American treaty rights.

Moreover, while water has always been scarce in the American West, and western policy makers have had to take that fact into account, other parts of the country have also been experiencing water shortages in the past five years, even the normally wet South. We need to continue to discover ways to resolve (or avoid) future water wars, especially in light of global climate change and its probable impact on world water supplies.

Part I

The Truckee and Carson River Basins

Chapter One

Water, People, and Politics

No issue in the American West captures public attention more than water. Attitudes about water in the West have been shaped by more than one hundred years of competition over this scarce resource. Debates about water policy therefore tend to be highly charged and deeply personal. This is not surprising to those who live in the West or are familiar with its landscape. The majority of western states receive less than twenty inches of precipitation each year. In the "wet" East, irrigation of cropland is not necessary; in the dry West, crops would not survive without it. Average annual precipitation in Nevada is less than ten inches, making it the driest state in the Union. In west-central Nevada, where the Carson, Truckee, and Walker River Basins are located, annual precipitation averages less than five inches. Moreover, all three rivers are overallocated, meaning that water rights holders are entitled (on paper) to more water than can actually be delivered.

The Great Basin, in which most of the state of Nevada is located, is an immense expanse that includes most of northern Nevada, half of Utah, and parts of California, Oregon, Idaho, and Wyoming. The Great Basin is a land of "interior drainage" because the rivers run inland toward lakes or sinks. None of the surface waters ever reaches the ocean or sea. In addition, the Sierra Nevada mountain range, with peaks reaching ten to twelve thousand feet, blocks many of the rain- and snowstorms from the Pacific Coast that otherwise might reach Nevada.

A key feature of three of northern Nevada's major river systems —Truckee, Carson, and Walker—is that each originates in California, outside the Great Basin. The Truckee River rises from Lake

Tahoe—its major water source—and flows approximately 120 miles, through the Truckee Meadows. The Truckee River historically terminated in Pyramid Lake, but since completion of Derby Dam in 1905, more than half (and sometimes all) of the flows of the Truckee River have been diverted to the Lahontan Reservoir in Churchill County, where it has been used, along with Carson River water, for irrigated agriculture.

The Carson River rises in the high Sierra Nevada in Alpine County, California. Its east fork originates on the slopes of Sonora Peak, at eleven thousand feet; the west fork originates near Carson Pass. The two forks of the Carson River flow north to cross the Nevada border and merge in the Carson Valley, where the water is used to irrigate farmlands in Carson City and Churchill and Douglas Counties. The Carson River naturally flowed 180 miles into the Carson Sink. However, starting in 1915, the waters of the Carson River have been captured and stored in Lahontan Reservoir.

The Walker River originates on the Sierra Crest's western boundary of Yosemite National Park. Through its two forks, the East and the West, it winds its way through mountain valleys and canyons along the California (Mono County)–Nevada border to Smith and Mason Valleys. The two forks merge 5 miles south of Yerington, becoming the main-stem Walker River. By the time the two forks merge, the volume of each has been greatly diminished, having been used to support extensive irrigated agriculture in the Mason and Smith Valleys, in Lyon County. The river then passes by ranches and farms surrounding Yerington, through a state wildlife refuge and Lahontan cutthroat trout hatchery, across the boundary of the Walker River Paiute Reservation, and into Walker Lake. The reservation and the lake are located in Mineral—not Lyon—County. Besides sharing these three rivers, California and Nevada also share Lake Tahoe. One-third of the lake lies on the Nevada side of the border; the rest is in California.

Many attempts have been made to resolve water conflicts in the West, with mixed results. In large part, this is because of the way in which water policy developed during early settlements of the West.

The Early Years

The first major use of water in the West was for mining, followed by irrigated agriculture. Both uses require the removal of water from the streambed, applying the water, and returning what is left to the river. These "return flows" tend to be far less than the amount originally diverted. The fact that mining and agriculture were the earliest economic uses to which water was put in the West gave rise to the three major principles of the "prior appropriation doctrine," the dominant water allocation and use principle in the West; these are the priority rule, the diversionary requirement, and the beneficial-use requirement. All seventeen western states adopted the prior appropriation doctrine, including Nevada.

The priority rule states that the first person to divert water from a stream has the prior right to use the water: "First in time, first in right." Thus, users of appropriative water are classified according to the verifiable dates on which each began to use the water. The earliest priority must be satisfied, or "made whole," before the next claimant can use any water. In times of shortage, the low-priority (junior) users may be required to reduce operations or to cease them altogether.

The diversionary requirement that a "valid" use must entail the physical removal of water from the stream resulted from the fact that the first major and competitive water uses were associated with diversionary activities. Appropriated water must also be put to a "beneficial" use within a given amount of time. Failure to do so may result in a challenge to or loss of the right to use the water. Historically, "beneficial" use has been defined in economic terms; noneconomic uses of water (for example, recreation) were denied in favor of mining and agriculture. Beneficial uses originated in common law but were eventually incorporated into statutory law. (Common law is the traditional law of an area or region, based on custom and court-derived precedent.)

The ultimate result of these principles has been the development of a "consumptive" ideology, which historically perpetuated the notions that water not used is wasted or lost; only economic, diversionary uses are beneficial; and individuals have the right, if all other requirements are met, to use the allotted amount of water no matter what conditions prevail—even to the detriment of other users or the surrounding environment. Adding to the culture of consumption is the requirement that if a water rights holder does not continuously use the water for defined beneficial purposes, those rights may be considered abandoned or forfeited.

The appropriation doctrine worked rather well during its early years, largely because there was little competition for that water outside mining and agriculture. However, that doctrine does not readily accommodate newer uses and users. It also discourages the conservation of water supplies. For example, employing more efficient irrigation methods or moving to less water-intensive crops might result in the loss of rights to use the amount of water that is saved, under the "use it or lose it" principle.

Early Conflicts

The first major series of water disputes between California and Nevada arose in the mid-nineteenth century, when Nevada questioned the right of private interests to draw off the waters of Lake Tahoe to encourage and support growth in Northern California. Although each state controlled individual water rights within its borders, the disposition of their shared waters was uncertain. Eventually, the courts became involved, resulting in numerous agreements and decrees to govern the use of the waters of Lake Tahoe and the Truckee, Carson, and Walker River systems. None of these provided any definitive, long-term solutions to issues of water allocation and use in either state, however. In the early 1950s, the two states entered negotiations on an interstate compact that would allocate the waters of the three rivers—and Lake Tahoe—once and for all time. It took more than fourteen years to reach such an agreement. The California-Nevada Interstate Compact Concerning the Waters of Lake Tahoe, Truckee River, Carson River, and Walker River Basins was finalized on June 25, 1968, and ratified by California in 1970 and Nevada in 1971.

Both states lobbied for and expected congressional approval, but Congress withheld it. From 1971 to 1979, Nevada and California congressional delegations proposed six separate bills seeking ratification; none even received a hearing. One final major effort was made by Senator Paul Laxalt of Nevada in 1985. Although a hearing was held on the bill he introduced, the bill never became law.[1] This was because the compact left too many issues unresolved. Since that time, in a show of mutual trust and support, both California and Nevada have retained the provisions of the compact in their respective laws and agreed to abide by those terms at the state level.

Reasons for Failure

The failure of various parties to obtain ratification of the compact for more than fifteen years was largely because the versions of the compact submitted to Congress emphasized the protection of the water rights of those who negotiated it; alternative points of view were not included. In particular, Article 1 of the compact ("Purposes") stated the following: "Consistent with the provisions of the authorization Acts of the State of California and the State of Nevada and the United States, the major purposes of this compact *are* to provide for the equitable apportionment of water between the two states; to protect and enhance *existing* economies; to remove causes of *present and future* controversies; to permit the *orderly integrated and comprehensive* development, use, conservation and control of the water within the Lake Tahoe, Truckee River, Carson River, and Walker River Basins" (emphasis added). The prior appropriation doctrine, which is the predominant water use doctrine of most western states, has that bias built into it: to protect the status quo.

In addition, the terms of the compact attempted to constrain the federal government. Historically, interstate compacts that address tribal water rights have included language that essentially indemnifies the United States and its Indian wards; in other words, the agreement that is reached has no binding effect on the federal government. In contrast, the California-Nevada compact included language that would specifically bind the US government to the terms of the agreement if it were ratified. Specifically, "Congress provides in its consent legislation that . . . the . . . provisions of the compact shall be binding on the agencies, wards, and instrumentalities of the United States of America."[2]

Another hindrance came from the rise of the Indian rights movement in the 1960s and 1970s. This movement emerged in the late 1960s in the wake of the fishing rights struggles of tribes in the Pacific Northwest that began in 1965. The 1969–71 occupation of Alcatraz Island by the San Francisco–area Indians of the All Tribes Coalition "marked the beginning of a national Indian activist movement . . . that kept national [and eventually international] attention on Indian rights and grievances."[3] Alcatraz historically had been used by Native Americans in the Bay Area as a camping spot, as a place to harvest fish and bird eggs, and as a haven for Indians wishing to get away from the Spanish missionaries. Once the federal government converted it to a prison, many of its inmates were Native American. Thus, the island was a symbol of oppression of Native Americans by Anglos. The occupation of Alcatraz sparked Native American protests and activities and caught the attention of the American Indian Movement.

AIM was founded in 1968 in Minneapolis, Minnesota, by a group of urban Chippewa Indians, led by Dennis Banks, George Mitchell, and Vernon and Clyde Bellecourt. AIM was created to focus attention on the abuse of Indians at the hands of the local police and to advocate programs for Indian housing, jobs, and education. After meeting with the Indians occupying Alcatraz during the summer of 1970, AIM came to understand the value of activism—and began organizing protests.

AIM's first national protest occurred on Thanksgiving Day 1970, when AIM members took over the Mayflower II in Plymouth, Massachusetts, to protest the celebration of "discovery" of a "new world," when that world was already occupied. The Indian rights movement embraced what turned out to be very successful tactics such as focusing media and public attention on Indian issues, collaborating with other Indian organizations in pursuit of common goals, demanding fulfillment of treaty rights, reasserting Native spiritual and cultural traditions, and, eventually, working with the United Nations in the pursuit of decolonization and self-determination for indigenous peoples all over the world. It focused national—and international—attention on the plight of Native Americans throughout the 1970s. Their accomplishments continue to be embraced—and extended—by succeeding generations.[4] As a consequence of this movement, Native American tribes became able to influence water policy in the American West. When the Native American rights movement was at its zenith, the Pyramid Lake Paiute Tribe vehemently opposed the compact—and its collective voice was ultimately heard.

Another factor in the failure to ratify the compact was the environmental movement, which raised public consciousness of the values associated with recreation, fish, and wildlife and enhanced public awareness of the impact of water development projects on these values. In the West, this has translated into recognition that irrigated agriculture has been a significant "environmental offender" in its own right. For example, agriculture is a principal source of nonpoint pollution. The long-term effects of pesticides, fertilizer, and trace elements in drainage and return flows were beginning to be recognized. Environmental groups, armed with environmental laws and court precedents, became much more effective at ensuring that those impacts would be addressed.

Throughout the 1960s and 1970s, Congress passed a host of laws designed to put into place national environmental protections to clean up the damage that had already been done and to prevent further degradation. All of these laws were passed with little opposition. Although the election of Ronald Reagan in 1980 might have signaled the end of the environmentalism of the 1970s, the laws and the bureaucratic machinery to carry them out have for the most part remained. Although many of these acts were amended in various ways in the late twentieth and early twenty-first centuries, environmentalism has become part of mainstream American culture.

Two of northern Nevada's lakes—Pyramid and Walker—had been drastically affected by the use of more than 80 percent of the surface waters of the Truckee, Carson, and Walker Rivers for irrigated agriculture in the region. Pyramid and Walker are two of the six large desert terminal lakes in western North America. They also are two of the three desert terminal lakes in this area that contain a freshwater fishery. (The third is Summit Lake, also located in Nevada.) The natural terminus of the Truckee River is Pyramid Lake. Because much of the Truckee River had been diverted to augment water supplies for irrigated agriculture, by 1966 the level of Pyramid Lake had dropped by 80 feet, exposing sandbars at the mouth of the Truckee River; a delta began to form between the lake and the river, making it increasingly difficult for fish to spawn. After passage of the Endangered Species Preservation Act of 1966 (PL 89-669), the Lahontan cutthroat trout (Oncorhynchus clarki heshawi) and the cui-ui (Chasmistes cujus), both found at Pyramid Lake, were listed as threatened and endangered, respectively. Indeed, cui-ui are found nowhere else in the world. This enabled the Pyramid Lake Paiute Tribe to argue aggressively for obtaining more water for the lake. Also by 1966, the Walker Lake level had dropped 108 feet. This, coupled with greatly increased levels of total dissolved solids (TDS), threatened the lake's viability as a fishery. Moreover, Nevada was experiencing rapid growth. In the case of the Carson and Truckee Rivers, demands were being made by the local water purveyor, Westpac Utilities (now the Truckee Meadows Water Authority), for increased storage capacity for use in times of drought. Demands were also being made by environmentalists for the preservation, enhancement, and maintenance of both lakes.

By the time the compact was submitted to Congress, the above effects indicated that new ways to address water resources allocation and uses in the West were needed. Realizing this, Congress declined to ratify the compact.

However, beginning in 1986, newly elected Nevada senator Harry Reid revived the idea of an interstate compact. He focused his attention only on the Carson and Truckee Rivers, noting that the parties in those conflicts seemed finally ready to negotiate solutions to problems associated with the first reclamation project ever constructed in the West: the Newlands Project, located in north-central Nevada. That project had generated more than one hundred years of litigation, much of which involving the federal government. It wanted not only to disentangle itself from those lawsuits, but also to help the parties reach an agreement that would end the water "wars" in which they had been engaged for decades—and that would also pass congressional "muster." Reid hoped that the end result would be the preservation and maintenance of Pyramid Lake.

Senator Reid had several reasons for refraining from including the Walker River Basin in his early efforts to end the water wars in northern Nevada. The parties in the Walker Basin were not as ready to negotiate as were those in the Carson and Truckee River Basins. Indeed, a 2003 court-mandated mediation among the parties produced no agreement. Reid believed that the situation in the Walker River Basin was distinct enough that it should be tackled at another time, using a different process. He initiated the Walker Basin Project in 2005.

By the turn of the twentieth century, it seemed that although the negotiated settlement process had yielded some success stories, the federal government had several reasons for seeking different means to resolve water resource conflicts in which it was a party. The settlement process did not always work as well as anticipated in all cases. The outcomes of some of these negotiations have been subject to criticism, especially in those cases involving Native American tribes that seemed to have been dealt, once again, the short end of the stick.

The approach taken in the Walker Basin is one of those ways. The Walker Basin Project embraces a different, private-sector-oriented approach to resolving water resource conflicts. The approach taken in the Walker Basin involves a scientifically driven effort to purchase enough water from willing sellers in the basin to "save" Walker Lake, while minimizing or mitigating economic and ecological impacts to the region.

Chapter Two

Reclamation Policy—
Trials and Tribulations

Irrigation of the arid West was established long before the national government became involved in promoting it. The first nonnative irrigation ditches appeared in Nevada in the early 1850s, diverting water from many Nevada streams onto farmland and pastures to supplement family gardens, grow hay, and support ranching activities. In 1870 the California Legislature authorized the Donner Lumber and Boom Company to construct a dam at the outlet of Lake Tahoe to control its outflow into the Truckee River. Through the latter part of the 1800s, the area around the Truckee River continued to grow. Such growth was supported by increasing the number of dams and diversions for a variety of purposes: to irrigate agriculture, generate electricity, power mills, and supply farmers with water for domestic use.

The earliest priority rights along these ditches and streams date to 1861. In addition, in 1866 the Nevada Legislature approved the construction of a bulkhead on the Carson River that essentially split it into three main channels. Each channel supported a network of small dams and canals for irrigation and other purposes. By 1870 Churchill County had thirty-six working ranches. As the area continued to grow throughout the 1880s and 1890s, the Nevada Legislature was urged to support the construction of large irrigation projects on the Truckee and Carson Rivers, but it declined to do so.

In the mid-1800s, individuals and families began to head westward by the thousands. Because 90 percent of the US population lived east of the 100th meridian, where conditions were extremely crowded, there was a concerted effort by the national government to encourage this migration. Average annual precipitation east of the 100th meridian is twenty inches or more, which spares farmers from having to irrigate their crops. West of the 100th meridian, average annual precipitation is ten inches or less. This is insufficient to sustaining farming. Thus, the only way that these increasing populations would survive in the arid and semiarid western environment was through the eventual support of irrigated farming by the federal government.

The great appeal of federally sponsored irrigation was that it offered something for both the East and the West. It promised "land for the landless, the redistribution of surplus workers, new markets for eastern manufacturers and railroads, the shoring up of cherished American values, and even a laboratory for the construction of model rural communities."[1]

For more than twenty-five years, reclamation "pioneers" had pushed the national government to embrace western reclamation. Prominent among them was Francis G. Newlands, who believed that reclamation was the "highest form" of conservation.[2] An attorney who moved from California to Nevada in 1888, he served as a Democrat in the US House of Representatives from 1893 to 1903. He believed that because water did not recognize state boundaries, reclamation must be subject to federal authority and regulation if it was to succeed. However, congressional Republicans and the administration of President William McKinley remained staunchly against federally sponsored reclamation, in spite of increased pressure from the popular press, railroad interests, and western congressmen, which intensified during the economic depression of the 1890s.[3]

After President McKinley's assassination and death on September 14, 1901, the situation changed dramatically. Theodore Roosevelt became president and ushered in a "democratic movement supporting 'the greatest good for the greatest number,' and, among other things, public ownership of utilities, an income tax, and support of labor and agriculture."[4] Roosevelt's first annual address to Congress, on December 1, 1901, proposed that reclamation be supported by the federal government. He also persuaded reluctant eastern legislators to support reclamation legislation.

On January 7, 1902, a reclamation bill was introduced in the Senate by Henry C. Hansbrough of North Dakota. Newlands introduced the bill in the House on that same day. Roosevelt issued a plea to members of both the House and the Senate to pass the bill. The thorniest issue was to what extent Congress should permit state involvement and control. Roosevelt insisted that the irrigation works be built by the federal government and that "distribution of the water, the diversion of the streams among irrigators, should be left to the settlers themselves, in conformity with State laws and without interference with those laws or with vested rights."[5] Consequently, the bill was passed by both houses.

The Reclamation Act

The Reclamation Act became law on June 17, 1902. The United States Reclamation Service (renamed the Bureau of Reclamation in 1923), created by the act and located in the Department of the Interior, assumed control of and responsibility for reclamation in the seventeen western states.

Because the initial reclamation project sites were to be chosen based on which states first passed enabling legislation, Nevada moved swiftly to make this happen. The Irrigation Act was passed by the Nevada Legislature in early 1903 to promote the state's cooperation with the Department of the Interior on the project. This act also required the documentation of existing water rights on the Truckee and Carson River systems, which had to occur before the project could move forward. Accordingly, the act created the State Engineer's Office and required, among other things, that the engineer prepare a list of all appropriations from every stream in the state in order of priority date. A certificate was issued to each water user certifying those rights.

The Newlands Project

The Truckee-Carson Irrigation Project (renamed the Newlands Project in 1919) was authorized on March 14, 1903, and construction began September 11. The Derby Diversion Dam on the Truckee River was completed in June 1905. Settlement of the irrigated land was encouraged by the Homestead Act, which offered 160 acres of land to those individuals who wanted to settle it. Much land had already been withdrawn from the public domain in order to make as much land as possible open for individual settlement in the project area.

Because the waters of the Carson River alone were not sufficient to irrigate the acreage thought to be arable at that time (400,000–500,000 acres), a substantial amount of Truckee River water was diverted at Derby Dam via the 32.5-mile Truckee Canal for the irrigation of the land around Fernley, Hazen, and Swingle Bench, Nevada, and to augment the flow of the Carson River in Lahontan Valley, Churchill County. The Lahontan Reservoir was completed in 1915, and the waters of the Carson River and diversions from the Truckee River began to be stored there. The project was divided into two parts: the Truckee Division to the north, near Fernley, to irrigate the lands along the Truckee Canal, and the Carson Division, to irrigate land in and around Fallon, Nevada, in Lahontan Valley. From 1906 to 1968, Truckee River water diverted at Derby Dam to the Carson River Basin averaged 250,000 acre-feet per year (a-f-y).[6] An acre-foot is that amount of water it takes to fill an acre of land with 1 foot of water.

In the years following, that number rose to 406,000; indeed, at times, all of the waters of the Truckee River were diverted. The decision to use Truckee River water in an interbasin transfer to augment the water that would be available to Newlands Project irrigators eventually came to plague the project—and everyone associated with it—for decades to come. At the time, however, there was much optimism.

The area that would become part of the Newlands Project was selected for a variety of reasons, perhaps the most important being that one of its principal water sources (the Truckee River) originated in a massive natural reservoir: Lake Tahoe. A small dam on the Truckee River outlet to Lake Tahoe controls the top 6.1 feet of the lake (above the natural rim of the lake) and provides 744,600 a-f of storage. When the lake's elevation is higher than its natural rim, water is released from the lake into the Truckee River. In dry years, Lake Tahoe drops below its natural rim, permitting no water to reach the gates at the dam. Whenever severe drought occurred during the early years of the project, water was actually pumped from the lake into the Truckee River, a practice opposed by California and Lake Tahoe landowners. This matter was settled by the Truckee River Agreement of 1935, which specified the conditions under which water could be pumped from the lake when it was at or below its natural rim.

At first, the water diverted from the Truckee at Derby Dam was dumped directly into the Carson River. Because of frequent water shortages, it became apparent that a major storage facility was needed. Multiple storage sites along the Truckee and Carson Rivers were considered, but ultimately a site in the Newlands Project area was selected. Lahontan Dam and Reservoir was constructed toward the end of the Carson River in 1915 to store water for use in the irrigation season. The reservoir is long and narrow, follows the contours of the river, and has a storage capacity of 300,000 a-f. The diversion canal was eventually rerouted to empty into the reservoir. Lahontan Dam itself is a 162-foot earth-fill dam. To prevent seepage, a cutoff wall extends 30–60 feet below the ground surface and 6–8 feet above the surface, into the embankment. With a hydroelectric plant immediately downstream from the dam, Lahontan Reservoir supplied electricity to rural agricultural areas. The power plant was constructed by the Truckee Carson Irrigation District (TCID) to supply power to the growing towns of Fallon and Stillwater. The reservoir captures the entire flow of the Carson River, plus the water diverted from the Truckee River at Derby Dam.

Water is released from the dam into a network of canals operated by the TCID, which contracts with the Bureau of Reclamation for Newlands Project waters. The completion of Lahontan Dam essentially finished the construction phase of the Newlands Project. The Lake Tahoe and Lahontan reservoirs initially served as the two main storage facilities on the system. Although it was estimated at the time that more than 500,000 acres could be brought into cultivation, the irrigated acreage never exceeded 73,000. In recognition of the limitations of the project, the maximum number of acres that could be served by the project was set at 74,500 in 1926.[7] The district boundaries in both Churchill and Lyon Counties include 120,000 acres, 73,000 of which have water rights.

Completion of the Newlands Project aggravated water allocation and use conflicts between the states of Nevada and California and among users in each state. Eventually, the courts became involved, resulting in a series of agreements and decrees to govern the use of the waters of Lake Tahoe and the Truckee and Carson River systems. The following is a brief overview of the most significant of these decisions.

The Truckee River General Electric Decree

One of the earliest of these conflicts was over control of the dam at the outlet of Lake Tahoe. The US Reclamation Service, despite having claims to water stored in Lake Tahoe, could not guarantee delivery of that water to Derby Dam unless it had control of the outlet dam at Lake Tahoe, which at the time was owned by the Tahoe Boom and Logging Company. Beginning in 1902, Reclamation began negotiations with the logging company for purchase of its dam. Before the negotiations were completed, the logging company sold it to the Truckee River General Electric Company for $40,000. In 1903 the electric company offered the dam to Reclamation for $100,000, which the secretary of the interior deemed too expensive. In 1904 Reclamation purchased a 63-acre site just downstream from the existing dam for construction of a new dam. When construction began in 1905, the electric company obtained an injunction to halt it. In the following year, the company offered control, but not ownership, of the dam for $50,000, if Reclamation guaranteed flows of 400 cubic feet per second from the first of October through the end of February and 500 cfs from March to September (1 cfs is 2 a-f per day). The company needed these flows to generate electricity year-round. Once again Interior declined the offer. Then, in 1909, Reclamation filed a condemnation suit against the company.

This suit became United States v. The Truckee River General Electric Company, et al. The court's decision, rendered on June 4, 1915, constituted the Truckee River General Electric Decree (known as the Truckee River Decree). It concluded that the power company owned the dam, the land around it, and rights to 500 cfs in the summer and 400 cfs during the winter as measured at Floriston, California. That geographical point was chosen because in 1908, the Truckee River General Electric Company entered into an agreement with the Floriston Pulp and Paper Company and the Floriston Land and Power Company (all three of which used the waters of the Truckee River in their operations) to ensure adequate flows to generate power year-round. These "Floriston" rates were for the release of water from Tahoe Dam into the Truckee River. The electric company owned the outlet dam at Lake Tahoe when it entered into agreement with the Floriston Land and Power Company to provide the Floriston rates. Thus, this agreement was incorporated into the Truckee River Decree. In essence, then, water releases from the Lake Tahoe dam were based on the requirement that water be released into the Truckee River to generate year-round electrical power, a fact that became critical to understand (and to change) decades later. This is because the water release schedule for the Truckee River could not be altered with this requirement in place.

No change of title occurred for the dam, but Reclamation purchased an easement for control and use of the dam for $139,500. It also provided half of the cost of construction of a new dam at Tahoe City. In the end, Reclamation had control of the dam at the outlet of Lake Tahoe and consequently control of the amount of water that was emptied, in high-water years, into the Truckee River from Lake Tahoe. This, in turn, enabled Reclamation to move water down the Truckee River, where much of it was diverted at Derby Dam to serve project irrigators.

The Orr Ditch Decree

In 1913 Reclamation decided that it needed to know which users were entitled to how much water and for what uses. It also needed clarification of firm water rights for both the Newlands Project and irrigation on the Pyramid Lake Paiute Reservation. The reservation constitutes 475,000 acres (742.2 square miles), which includes the 112,000 acres that cover the surface of Pyramid Lake, which is fifteen miles long and eleven miles wide.

The United States thus filed an allegedly "friendly" lawsuit for adjudication of all water rights on the Truckee River. The suit, United States v. Orr Water Ditch Company, et al. had as defendants not only the water company but every water rights owner on the Truckee River, its tributaries, and all ditches. The federal government sought enough water for the Newlands Project to irrigate 230,000 acres, which is four times as much as the project has ever irrigated. The court finally issued the Orr Ditch Decree (as it came to be called) thirty-one years later, in 1944.[8]

This decree gave legal sanction to the major elements of the Truckee River Decree, including the section dealing with Floriston rates. It also awarded the federal government a 1902 priority right to divert Truckee River water at Derby Dam at the rate of 1,500 cfs. The water was to be used for irrigating farmland in the Newlands Project, storage in Lahontan Reservoir, and the generation of power and other municipal and domestic purposes. The Sierra Pacific Power Company (SPPCO) was granted the right to use approximately 29,000 a-f of water per year for municipal, industrial, and domestic purposes in the metropolitan area of Reno-Sparks.[9]

The federal government also received water rights for the irrigation of 5,875 acres on the Pyramid Lake Reservation (30,000 a-f). These water rights were granted a priority date of 1859 (the year in which the reservation was created). The federal government resisted the urgings of the Bureau of Indian Affairs to obtain "reserved" water rights for the reservation, a legal concept that was established in 1908 by the US Supreme Court.

In that case, Winters v. United States, the Court prohibited any non-Indian water use that would interfere with a tribe's use of its water rights, which included "reserved" water rights.[10] This is because when a reservation was established, the federal government implicitly reserved, in addition to the land, water rights sufficient to meet the purposes for which the reservation was created. These water rights had a priority right dating back to the year in which a given reservation was created. In theory, this doctrine gave the Pyramid Lake Paiute Reservation the most senior (1859) water rights on the system and entitled it to enough water to meet its agricultural needs and to maintain Pyramid Lake.

The federal government later petitioned the Court to reopen the Orr Ditch Decree so that the issue of reserved water rights for the Pyramid Lake Paiute Tribe could be addressed. The Court rejected that plea, bringing into question the tribe's ability to pursue additional water for the lake under the Winters Doctrine.[11]

The Truckee Carson Irrigation District

Reclamation assured Newlands Project farmers that adequate water for irrigation would be delivered, that satisfactory drainage could be provided by the ditches that were excavated in 1906, that the soil was fertile, and that markets existed for their produce. These assurances constituted serious misjudgments by Reclamation. The farmers soon discovered that a 160-acre farm was too small to provide an adequate income in a climate where precipitation was so erratic and where a day's windstorms could undo a season's worth of leveling and grading. That the topsoil was thin, hardpan, and near the surface only worsened the situation because it created drainage problems.

By 1908, many areas were already becoming waterlogged. By 1912, "Large areas on the project were saturated and unusable. Drainage ditches excavated in 1906 did not sufficiently drain irrigated fields, and the water table was very near the surface, saturating the root zone."[12] That same year, the farmers demanded that Reclamation construct deep drains. However, Reclamation responded that it was not responsible for drains or drainage and that the farmers should bear the costs of constructing and maintaining their own drains. The farmers then aligned themselves into a more formal— and permanent—organization, an idea that Reclamation had long supported. They assessed themselves five cents per acre and joined the National Federation of Water Users' Associations. The Nevada Legislature passed an enabling act in March 1917, authorizing the creation of an irrigation district. Churchill County commissioners ordered that an election be held on November 16, 1917, to determine whether project farmers were in favor of creating a water district. The farmers' representatives voted nine to one in favor of the measure. The Truckee Carson Irrigation District was chartered as a political subdivision of the state of Nevada in the following year.

Perhaps to ease tensions and promote growth on its already costly project, Reclamation proposed to begin work on a drainage system—this being the most serious of the problems facing the farmers—as soon as a contract could be negotiated regarding payment for the costs of construction. A contract was approved in 1921, followed by a second contract in 1924. By 1928 the work was complete, and more than 230 miles of drains had been excavated, after which drainage was no longer a serious problem.[13]

During the early years, the Newlands Project operators struggled to meet the needs of project farmers. When Reclamation opened lands for settlement in 1904, 800 farm sites were available. During the first irrigation season of 1905, only 108 had been settled. Even by 1908, only 300 had been settled. In 1910 project lands were closed to new settlement because water was insufficient to irrigate even the land that had been cultivated. Since the Carson River emptied into a sink at that time, Reclamation and TCID decided to capture and store the water before it entered the sink. When Lahontan Dam was completed in 1915, the Newlands Project was reopened to settlement. At that time, 571 farms were being cultivated. That number increased to 648 by 1918 and 906 in 1922.[14] At last, the project began to produce what it had promised: water for irrigation, settlement, and livelihood. In 1911 the Warren Act permitted reclamation water to be sold to private landowners, increasing the value of land in the area. The private parties could either purchase water directly from Reclamation or join the Newlands Project.

After World War I ended, conditions on Reclamation projects in the West had deteriorated to the point that inconsistent delivery of water to public lands resulted in farmers' profits being insufficient to repay Reclamation for the costs of construction. The secretary of the interior appointed a fact-finding commission, which determined, in the case of the Newlands Project, that $7,899,470 had been spent on it. Of that amount, more than $4 million had been spent improperly. The commission decided that the project users did not have to repay that money. The 1926 Omnibus Adjustment Act gave project water users forty years to repay the difference, which turned out to be $3,287,999.

On December 31, 1926, Reclamation entered into a contract with TCID that assigned TCID the responsibility to operate all facets of the project. Under this agreement, Reclamation was obligated to deliver to the Newlands Project 406,000 a-f of water for the irrigation of a maximum of 74,500 acres. TCID also assumed responsibility for the Tahoe, Derby, Lahontan, and Carson Diversion Dams. The Carson Diversion Dam feeds water from Lahontan Reservoir into the project's main distribution canals.[15] With this contract, the farmers finally gained more control over the project.

The Truckee River Agreement

Even before the formation of TCID, there was a pressing need for additional storage capacity on the Truckee River. By the 1930s, Washoe County boasted a population of 27,158. Reno and Sparks continued to grow as an agricultural and ranching area. The population of Churchill County had grown to 5,075.[16] The fish populations in Pyramid Lake had begun to decline dramatically because the lake level had dropped precipitously. Winnemucca Lake completely disappeared. Meanwhile, the Orr Ditch adjudication, which was intended to direct the regulation of the water system of the Truckee River, would remain in the courts for more than fifteen years.

The need for additional storage capacity, coupled with a desire to better regulate the system, led to the Truckee River Agreement of 1935. The agreement was signed by the federal government, Truckee Carson Irrigation District, Washoe County Water Conservation

District, and Sierra Pacific Power Company. The agreement formally recognized the natural rim of Lake Tahoe at 6,223 feet, providing for 6.1 feet of storage above the rim, which translated into a 744,600 a-f storage capacity. It also acknowledged that additional storage capacity was needed on the system and allocated $1 million to Reclamation for the construction of Boca Reservoir. The agreement incorporated a modified version of the Floriston rates requirement by allowing for reduced rates (below 400 cfs) when Lake Tahoe was below a certain elevation during the winter. It also included the terms of the Truckee River General Agreement, as well as the 1926 contract with TCID. The signatories also formally agreed to accept the terms of the Orr Ditch Decree, in advance of its being issued. This agreement is still in effect.

The Washoe Project

In the early 1950s, Reclamation investigated the possibility of building additional storage capacity along the Truckee and Carson Rivers. In December 1952, Reclamation issued a status report on three possible plans for development. The plan that would ultimately be adopted was outlined in a feasibility report issued in September 1954. The Washoe Project, as it came to be known, was authorized by Public Law 858 on August 1, 1956. Its purpose was to build additional reservoirs on the upper Truckee and Carson Rivers for "irrigation, municipal and industrial uses, recreation, power, flood control and restoration of Pyramid Lake fisheries."[17] The major features of the project included three dams: Prosser Creek, Stampede Reservoir, and Watasheamu Dam. The act authorizing the Washoe Project specifically directed that the facilities at Lake Tahoe provide for the increased water releases and restoration of the fishery. The act also authorized construction of Marble Bluff Dam and Fishway on the Truckee River, near Pyramid Lake. The House report on the Washoe Project stressed that the restoration of the lake's fish population "to its full potential is deemed to be of national interest and importance."[18]

In spite of such assurances, the Pyramid Lake Paiute Tribe

opposed the Washoe Project. By the time the Washoe Project was approved, Pyramid Lake had dropped more than 70 feet, largely caused by TCID's at times diverting almost the entire flow of the Truckee River to Lahontan Reservoir. The low water level resulted in the formation of a delta between the lake and the Truckee River, making spawning runs impossible for the lake's fish. By the mid- to late 1950s, both of the lake's fish species (cui-ui and Lahontan cut-throat trout) were headed toward extinction, which would be hastened by completion of the Washoe Project. The most objectionable part of the Washoe Project was Watasheamu Dam on the East Fork of the Carson River, which would enable greater upstream use of the water stored there to irrigate additional acreage. Water to irrigate those lands would need to be taken from the Truckee River. In addition, Stampede Reservoir, with 226,500 a-f of storage capacity, would impound all the water that Pyramid Lake had been receiving. If Stampede and Watasheamu were constructed and operated as planned, Pyramid Lake might cease to exist.

Because of the tribe's opposition, the secretary of the interior created a task force to prepare a report on the potential impacts of the Washoe Project if it were completed as proposed. Although the report noted that the major goal of the Washoe Project was to provide water to the Newlands Project for irrigation, it questioned the legality of TCID's use of water stored in Lahontan to generate electricity in the winter, when the water was not needed for irrigation. It did so by diverting Truckee River water to Lahontan Reservoir solely for power generation. TCID's decreed water rights were for agricultural purposes only. The water diverted from the Truckee during winter to generate electricity wound up flowing into the Stillwater National Wildlife Refuge, not on farmlands. The Pyramid Lake Tribe argued that this was indeed "illegal" and that the water should be permitted to flow to the lake rather than to generate winter electricity. Regardless, additional storage capacity was eventually built on the system, but the proposed Watasheamu Dam was never constructed.

By 1971 the following reservoirs had been built on the Truckee River (including those constructed prior to the 1935 agreement):

RESERVOIR	USABLE CAPACITY	OWNER
Lake Tahoe	744,600 a-f	Reclamation
Donner Lake	9,500 a-f	SPPCO
Boca Reservoir	41,100 a-f	Reclamation
Independence Lake	17,500 a-f	SPPCO
Prosser Creek	29,800 a-f	Reclamation
Stampede	226,500 a-f	Reclamation
Martis Creek	Flood Control	SPPCO

Source: California Department of Water Resources, Truckee River Atlas, 11.

When Stampede Reservoir was finally completed in 1970, it was dedicated to flood control, recreational purposes, and providing inflows to Pyramid Lake, a decision that was challenged in the 1980s.

The Carson River: Union Mill Cases

The first controversies over Carson River water began in the early 1860s, between farmers and ranchers and the Comstock mining and milling interests. The resulting litigation is collectively referred to as the Union Mill cases.[19] Logging enterprises also had an interest in the dispute, because they could float their logs down the river through Carson Valley as long as the mills received enough water to maintain their operations in Dayton Valley. This period of conflict lasted until the late 1890s, at the end of the Comstock era. There was no longer any need for the mills (and no need for hydropower to run the mills); thus, there was no need for the continual flow of water in the river.

At the beginning of the twentieth century, conflict began to arise among the different agricultural users. These conflicts arose because water supply was located in California, while most of the demand was in Nevada.

Alpine Decree

After completion of the Newlands Project, the federal government filed lawsuits to clarify water rights on both the Carson and the Truckee River systems. In the case of the Truckee, the lawsuit, U.S.

v. Orr Water Ditch, et al., was filed in 1913, leading ultimately to the Orr Ditch Decree of 1944. In the case of the Carson, U.S. v. Alpine Land and Reservoir Company, et al. was filed in 1925. The case was not decided for another fifty-five years, with the issuance of the Alpine Decree in 1980, making this the longest-lived water rights case in US history.

The Alpine Decree established water rights in the Newlands Project area according to whether the water was used to irrigate bench- or bottomlands.[20] For the Newlands Project area below Lahontan Reservoir in Churchill County, the decrees provided for a maximum water duty of 4.5 a-f-y for benchlands and 3.5 a-f-y for bottomlands. For lands above Lahontan Reservoir, the decree established maximum water duties of 4.5 a-f-y for bottomlands, 6.0 a-f-y for alluvial-fan lands, and 9.0 a-f-y for benchlands.[21] These water duties were based on the water requirements for alfalfa, which was the dominant, and most water-intensive, crop grown in Nevada at that time.

However, the decree did not allocate the waters of the Carson River between the two states, and neither state was a party to the decree. The Alpine Decree also established storage rights in the high alpine reservoirs in the upper Carson River, which were permitted to fill out of priority order, because the snow does not melt until the summer at those high elevations. Those reservoirs were also permitted to be filled more than once in a given irrigation season to extend the growing season. In order for TCID to more effectively manage the system, the branches and tributaries of the Carson River were divided into eight segments, each of which was regulated independently. According to the terms of the decree, water releases from the Alpine reservoirs are controlled by a federal water master located in Reno. In the lower Carson River Basin, releases of water from Lahontan Reservoir are controlled by TCID according to specific operating criteria.

Change in Northern Nevada

The 1940s witnessed dramatic changes in Nevada. The commencement of World War II brought an influx of soldiers, sailors, airmen, and civilian defense workers to the state. As with the rest of the West, the population of Nevada began to grow considerably, from 110,247 in 1940 to 285,278 in 1960. In the mid-twentieth century, both Nevada's and California's rapid population growth brought agricultural interests into direct conflict with urban interests.

In the early 1950s, the issue of allocation of shared water resources surfaced in California and Nevada. Each was worried that the other would take more than its fair share of the three rivers (Carson, Truckee, and Walker) and the one lake (Lake Tahoe) that they shared. Both sides came to realize that an interstate water compact was the only way to bring about a comprehensive water agreement.

Chapter Three

The California-Nevada Interstate Compact

Being eager to collaborate on an interstate compact, California and Nevada formed compact commissions in early 1955. On August 4 of that year, President Eisenhower signed legislation enabling the two states to begin negotiations. At the first meeting of the two state commissions on January 17, 1956, Hugh Shamberger, Nevada state engineer, noted that the group was facing a "unique situation" in attempting to negotiate a compact pertaining to three river systems and one interstate lake. He added that this group "within a few months, a year or so, will be able to come to agreement."[1]

Nonetheless, it took more than fourteen years of tense, frequently stalled negotiations before the two states reached an agreement, in 1969. The California-Nevada Interstate Compact was ratified by California in 1970 and Nevada in 1971. Both states pressed Congress to ratify the compact, but it declined to do so. From 1971 to 1979, Nevada and California congressional delegations proposed six bills seeking ratification, but none received a hearing. Since then, in a show of mutual trust and support, both California and Nevada have retained the provisions of the compact in their respective laws and agreed to abide by them. Nonetheless, this did not appease the various users of the waters of the Truckee and Carson Rivers. They wanted a permanent, binding agreement that was sanctioned by the federal government. Lawsuits were pending, and additional litigation seemed imminent.

The Laxalt Compact

During the 1980s, Senator Paul Laxalt of Nevada led another attempt to present a compact to Congress that *would* be ratified. In 1985

Laxalt announced that he would not seek reelection in 1986. He very much wanted to see the compact ratified by Congress before he left the Senate. This would be his swan song in the Senate and part of his legacy to the state of Nevada.

The Nevada congressional delegation at the time—Laxalt, Senator Chic Hecht, Congresswoman Barbara Vucanovich, and Congressman Harry Reid—issued a statement saying, "We believe this legislation will put to rest, once and for all, the myriad of disputes and court actions that have plagued northern Nevada for close to 70 years."[2] President Ronald Reagan and Laxalt had been governors of the states of California and Nevada, respectively, when the original compact was ratified by both states. According to Patricia Zell, Democratic staff director and chief counsel of the Senate Committee on Indian Affairs, "The conventional wisdom at the time was that given the alignment of those persons in those positions and the alignment of the political stars, it was thought that this would be the opportune time to have Congress ratify that compact."[3] Joe Ely, a member of the Pyramid Lake Paiute's tribal council during this period, believed that the time for a settlement had finally come. Litigation over water rights in northern Nevada had been preventing the tribe from "moving into the future"; so much time and resources had been spent on lawsuits that the tribe was unable to focus on other tribal issues, such as economic development. The compact sponsored by Laxalt basically stated that the tribe *would* agree to the compact, as well as to the development of a mechanism to settle the remaining issues that were not part of the compact. Although the tribe initially supported the legislation, a group of tribal members, who became convinced that the compact would do serious harm to the lake, forced a referendum. Support for the settlement was withdrawn. Ely, who went to Washington with the tribe's attorney, Robert Pelcyger, was to oppose the compact. However, Ely was also given latitude by the tribe, if the opportunity arose, to negotiate on the tribe's behalf.[4]

Ely Goes to Washington

When Ely and Pelcyger arrived in Washington, Laxalt asked to meet with them. Ely's description of the meeting is telling:

They took us into this room and had this long table, and we sat on one side and [Laxalt] sat on the opposite side right across from me. Barbara Vucano-vich was there, and Chic Hecht was there, and Harry Reid was there. Laxalt led a somewhat tense meeting. He told me that he wanted the Nevada-California Compact passed, and I broke in a couple of times and said, "Well, that's not acceptable to us. It would harm the lake and we'd be willing to negotiate some other deal that would replace the compact." And he said, "We're going to get this compact passed. Do you understand me?" And I looked at him, and he says, "Do you understand me? We are going to get it passed. Do you understand me?" And I looked at him. We were looking at each other in the eyes during this process, and I said, "Yes, I understand." And that was the end of the meeting.

The entire time Laxalt was issuing his "ultimatum," he was shaking his finger in Ely's face, which reinforced Ely's determination to kill the compact.[5]

Under Ely's leadership as tribal chair, a major effort was mounted to defeat the bill. It helped that the Department of the Interior, the Department of Justice, and the Bureau of Indian Affairs opposed the compact. A major problem with the proposed compact was that it omitted the traditional clause for interstate compacts, which stated that the terms of the compact would not impair the rights of the federal government or those of its Indian wards. Instead, it went in the opposite direction, asserting that ratification of the compact would mean that both the federal government and relevant Indian tribes would be bound by its provisions.

Ross Swimmer, the assistant secretary of Indian affairs at the time, was quite assertive in his opposition as well, even though this could have jeopardized his job. Senator Daniel Inouye (D-HI), chair of the Senate Indian Affairs Committee, was staunchly pro–Native American and was receptive to the tribe's concerns. He and his committee did not support the compact. The tribe also hired a first-class lobbying firm in Washington, DC, Wexler, Reynolds, Harrison, and Schule, to represent them—and held a Grateful Dead concert on the reservation to help pay for the cost.

The proposed legislation went to the Senate Judiciary Committee for review. Committee members Laxalt, Pete Wilson, and Hecht supported the bill. Senator Alan Cranston of California did not, because of the serious damage he believed would be done to the lake. His stand was courageous, given President Ronald Reagan's role in negotiating the original compact. According to Ely, Cranston was "unwavering in his opposition, which persuaded other Senate Democrats to oppose the bill as well."[6]

A New Strategy

When it seemed clear that the bill would never make it out of committee, Laxalt maneuvered the bill in a different direction. Because he served on the Senate Appropriations Committee, he was able to get a single line—without advance warning or even a hearing—inserted into the 1987 appropriations bill that simply said, "The California and Nevada Interstate Compact is hereby ratified." The appropriations bill, with the ratification language intact, passed out of the Senate Appropriations Committee and was headed to the Senate floor for a vote.[7]

Prior to the full Senate vote, Ely and Pelcyger persuaded Senator Mark Hatfield (R-OR), chair of the Senate Appropriations Committee, that ratifying the compact would have the potential to destroy Pyramid Lake. Pelcyger spoke of the meeting between the three of them:

We started off by saying, "Senator, this compact is evil. And it is an attempt to totally undermine the Pyramid Lake, the Pyramid Lake Paiute Tribe, [and] the Pyramid Lake Reservation." He said, "Do you mean to tell me that our President, Ronald Reagan, and my good friend Senator Laxalt engaged in such an effort when they were governors of their states and this is what Senator Laxalt now wants ratified?" We said, "That's exactly right, Senator."

And he said, "I can't believe that." And we said, "Well, that's what we're here to do, to show it to you." So we had a map, and we had [the] provisions of the compact. . . . And by the end of the time, he was just shaking his head.[8]

At the time of the Senate Appropriations Committee meeting, Hatfield was not aware of either the unusual binding clause in the compact or that the Judiciary Committee refused to send it forward. As chair of that committee, Hatfield was immersed in budgetary matters and took Laxalt at his word—that obstructionist bureaucrats in the executive branch were the only ones opposed to the bill.

According to Pelcyger, although the interval between when the bill was referred from the Senate Appropriations Committee and when the Senate voted did not allow the Pyramid Lake Tribe much time to mobilize support, Ely and Pelcyger nonetheless began meeting with as many senators and staff as they could. They developed an alternative proposal and distributed it. They printed flyers and handed them out. At the same time, the tribe's lobbying firm conducted a media campaign against the compact. There were editorials nationwide about the issue in the *Washington Post, New York Times, Philadelphia Enquirer,* and the *Eugene (OR) Register-Guard.* The press pilloried both Laxalt and Reagan, the latter because he was governor when the original compact was adopted by California and because he was perceived as a close friend of Laxalt.

Although Cranston was willing to oppose the compact and to urge Senate Democrats to do the same, he refused to debate the powerful and formidable Laxalt on the Senate floor. Another ally was Senator Bill Bradley (D-NJ), who was the chair of the Subcommittee on Water and Power within the Senate Energy and Natural Resources Committee. After reading the editorials and doing a preliminary investigation, he had one of his staff inform Pelcyger that he was willing to do whatever he could to stop the compact from becoming law.

Before the anticipated Senate floor debate between Bradley and Laxalt could take place, Laxalt and the tribe reached an agreement, at Hatfield's urging. Laxalt agreed to take out any language that would negatively affect the tribe and to provide a fifty-million-dollar compensation package. When Laxalt conveyed this to Joe Gremban, president of Sierra Pacific Power Company, and Roland Wester-gard, head of the Nevada Department of Conservation and Natural Resources, they both indicated they would prefer no compact at all to this version. Laxalt then withdrew the ratification provision from the appropriations bill.

Zell noted that this was perceived as quite a victory for "a smaller, almost insignificant interest in the political arena . . . that [it] was highly unusual that people would take up the cause of one or more Indian tribes, unless the interests of those tribes are aligned with the delegation from the state that represents them."[9] In this case, the opposite was true: the delegation supported the compact. Zell stated that she never would have imagined Joe Ely's leadership skills to emerge in such a strident and forceful manner at exactly the time when the situation in Washington called for those qualities. He was not afraid to sit down with anyone at any time to advance his agenda—defeating that compact. At the time, Ely was only twenty-five years old, high school educated, had been tribal chairman for less than a year, and had no Washington political experience at all.

The tribe and its lobbying firm were incredibly effective in edu-cating key players about the threat that the compact posed to Pyra-mid Lake and, by extension, to the two listed species that lived there. Zell considered this critical in turning back the rising tide against an array of forces that many observers thought could never be over-come. It was truly an extraordinary event that established the tribe's political clout regarding water rights.

Other Reasons for Nonratification

As mentioned in chapter 1, the failure to obtain ratification of the compact for more than fifteen years was because the versions of the compact submitted to Congress emphasized the protection of the water rights of those involved in negotiating it to the exclusion of other interests that were by then demanding inclusion. Most notably, these were Native American, environmental, and urban interests. Moreover, no provision was made for water to maintain Pyramid Lake and the fisheries it contained. This was despite the fact that diminishing lake levels had severely affected those fisheries; by the early 1960s, the lake level had dropped by eighty feet.

Pyramid Lake and its unique fish population were the tribe's main economic, cultural, spiritual, and aesthetic resource. The lake covers 50 percent of the reservation and is home to the Lahontan cutthroat trout and the prehistoric cui-ui fish. The latter species is found *only* in Pyramid Lake; it was listed as "endangered" in 1967 under the Endangered Species Preservation Act of 1966.[10] The LCT was listed as "threatened" in 1970. The lake's Anaho Island serves as America's largest white-pelican rookery; diminished lake levels permitted a "land bridge" to the island, endangering its pelicans and other wildlife, because it gave predators access to the island. The decreased volume of water in the lake, combined with increased salinity levels, threatened the lake's ability to support any aquatic life.

The compact recognized only those waters allocated by the Orr Ditch Decree of 1944, which limited tribal water rights to agricultural uses. Under the Winters Doctrine of 1908, the tribe might have been entitled to enough water to serve all the purposes for which the reservation was created—including maintenance of the lake. Those water rights, if obtained, would have a priority right date of 1859, predating the creation of the Newlands Project, as well as all of the other Truckee River irrigators.

The Winters Doctrine notes that the federal government is responsible for protecting the interests of Native American tribes. The federal government's failure to assert or adequately establish those rights, as occurred with the Pyramid Lake Paiute Tribe and the Orr Ditch Decree, does not necessarily extinguish them— indeed, the US Supreme Court asserted in 1983 that the Pyramid Tribe "retains a Winters' right, at least in theory, to water to maintain the fishery."[11] But such rights *would* be negated if Congress ratified an interstate compact that failed to allocate additional water for

Pyramid Lake. Such a circumstance did not escape the notice of the tribe.

Other factors came into play as well. One of the last things Secretary of the Interior Stewart Udall did before leaving office in 1969 was to write a letter to the Office of Management and Budget (OMB) that expressed the department's opposition to the compact, citing both the language that would commit the federal government to the terms of the compact and the impact it would have on Pyramid Lake if ratified unchanged. The Justice Department was vehemently opposed as well, as it was contrary to the interests of the federal government to bind itself to the terms of a state agreement.

Another cause had to do with the environment. By the time the compact was submitted to Congress, the federal government realized that the proposed terms of the compact would conflict with its efforts to secure enough water to repair the environmental damage caused by the Newlands Project, not only within the Pyramid Lake Paiute Reservation but elsewhere in the Truckee-Carson system.

The Truckee-Carson River system has historically supported extensive wetlands areas. It also lies on the eastern edge of the Pacific Flyway for migrating birds. More than four hundred thousand ducks, twenty-eight thousand geese, and fourteen thousand swans use the area in their annual migrations.[12] More than half of the Pacific Flyway canvasback duck population use these wetlands, which also support more than 50 percent of the North American long-billed dowitcher population. It is home to the largest breeding colony of white-faced ibis in North America. Bald eagles winter there. American white pelicans nest there.

Since the completion of the Newlands Project at the turn of the twentieth century, Nevada wetlands have been depleted by 85 percent (from approximately 113,000 acres to less than 15,000). In addition, the previously clean water supplies in the remaining wetlands have received agricultural runoff from irrigated acreage. As irrigation in the area becomes more efficient, agricultural drainage is reduced, with consequent reductions in water flows to the wetlands.

As the wetlands die off, naturally occurring trace elements (arsenic, boron, lithium) become more concentrated—and toxic. All forms of wildlife feeding in such areas would be poisoned. Action was needed to protect the wetlands.

Environmental harm caused by the Newlands Project had triggered litigation by the Pyramid Lake Paiute Tribe and the US government against TCID and virtually every other user of Truckee River water in both Nevada and California. The tribe had been winning some of these cases and was becoming increasingly successful in its efforts to increase flows to the lake.

One of these efforts occurred in 1967, in response to passage of the Endangered Species Preservation Act. The Department of the Interior issued Operating Criteria and Procedures for the Newlands Project, which set the maximum annual total irrigable project acreage at 74,500 acres and the maximum total water deliveries at 406,000 a-f.[13] Annual OCAPS were to be issued each year through 1973. The idea was to reduce incrementally the use of Truckee River water for the Newlands Project, so that more of the water would eventually reach Pyramid Lake.

In 1968 the tribe filed the first in a series of lawsuits based on the issuance of the 1967 OCAP, claiming that water was being wasted in the Newlands Project. The Newlands Project was one of the—if not the—most wasteful and inefficient reclamation projects in the country. Evaporation and seepage caused more than 45 percent of the diversions to fail to reach the fields, because most of the ditches were neither covered nor lined. According to Pelcyger, one of the most "notorious things that was happening on the system . . . was that the principal water supply for the Newlands came from the Carson River. The Truckee River was a *supplemental* supply, which logically should have meant that the Truckee River would be diverted only when the Carson River flows were insufficient to meet the needs of the project."[14]

Until 1967, when the first OCAP was promulgated, Truckee River water was diverted whenever there was water flowing in it. During the winter, when Lahontan Reservoir was full, TCID continued to divert water for hydroelectric power generation. This meant that TCID was using project water for purposes other than irrigation. The 1967 OCAP prohibited the use of project water for wintertime power generation. This lawsuit was adjudicated in 1973.[15]

This decision, popularly known as the Gesell Opinion, was based on an updated view of the Winters Doctrine and held that the secretary of the interior had a legal obligation to ensure that Pyramid Lake received enough water to protect it, because this was necessary to preserve the lake's fisheries. This decision contained new operating criteria for the Newlands Project, which called for incremental reductions in allowed diversions of water from the then current amount of 406,000 a-f to 350,000 a-f in 1973 and then to 288,129 a-f for the years 1974–84. Beyond 1984 an annual OCAP has been determined each year, based on the actual acreage under irrigation and production. It also required Reclamation to deliver to Pyramid Lake all Truckee River water in excess of valid Newlands Project water rights. If the provisions of the OCAPs were violated, the court asserted, the 1926 Reclamation contract with TCID would be terminated.

TCID continued diverting water above the allowed amount, and the secretary of the interior terminated the contract, as directed. In response, TCID appealed the decision in the Ninth Circuit Court of Appeals.[16] The secretary's right to terminate the contract was upheld.[17] TCID believed that its actions were justified based on a lawsuit filed in 1974 by the City of Fallon to prevent implementation of the 1973 OCAP, pending completion of an Environmental Impact Statement.[18] TCID claimed that "the United States and the Pyramid Tribe agreed not to implement the 1973 criteria until . . . an Environmental Impact Study (EIS) was completed. The United States and the Pyramid Lake Tribe [knew] that they agreed not to implement the 1973 operating criteria, but they brought the lawsuit anyway."[19] TCID continued to divert and use water as it had prior to the Gesell Opinion and the 1973 OCAP. In 1983 this case was dismissed, effectively eliminating TCID's justification for not adhering to the 1973 OCAP.

Secretary of the Interior Roger Morton notified TCID that "every acre-foot of excessive diversions of water, based on the 1973 OCAP and the Gesell opinion, would have to be returned to Pyramid Lake."[20] Over a fifteen-year period, the "illegally" diverted water amounted to more than 1 million a-f.[21] The tribe began to pursue restitution from TCID and Newlands Project irrigators for diversions from the Truckee that violated existing OCAPS, a pursuit sanctioned by the Ninth Circuit Court.[22] This case also upheld the 1973 OCAP. The court found that the water diverted above the 1973 OCAPshould be "repaid" to the tribe.

One of the greatest legal victories of the Pyramid Lake Paiute Tribe occurred in 1984, when a lawsuit filed in 1976 was finally decided.[23] Stampede Reservoir was originally intended to provide water storage, drought protection, flood control, and recreation. Secretary of the Interior Stuart Udall was under a great deal of pressure to enter into a contract with the Carson-Truckee Water Conservancy District to operate the reservoir for the benefit of Westpac Utilities, the major water purveyor in the Reno-Sparks area and a subsidiary of the Sierra Pacific Power Company. The Carson-Truckee Water Conservancy District was a public entity created to contract with the secretary of the interior regarding the operation of Stampede Reservoir. Udall decided that the reservoir would be used for recreation and flood control until the issue of water supplies to the lake was settled.

The water conservancy district sued the secretary to force him to enter into a contract with them for the operation of Stampede Reservoir. The decision was not at all what they had expected. The court mandated that the water stored in Stampede Reservoir was to be used *only* for the benefit of the endangered and threatened fish species in Pyramid Lake. That decision was challenged unsuccessfully.[24] This was a major—and precedent-setting—victory for the tribe. It also gave SPPCO, a powerful political player in water politics in northern Nevada, a reason to ally itself with the tribe. This eventually led to an agreement between the two parties that facilitated the negotiation of what became Public Law 101-618.

A final set of legal problems facing the federal government involved the Fallon Paiute Shoshone Tribe, which has lived in the Lahontan Basin and Stillwater marshes for thousands of years. In 1890, under the provisions of the General Allotment Act of 1887, 50 160-acre allotments of land were assigned to the tribe. In 1894 146 additional 160-acre parcels were dedicated to the tribe, resulting in more than 31,000 acres overall. Most of this acreage was located in what later became the Newlands Project area. Following the authorization of the Newlands Project, the government coaxed the tribe into entering into contracts, in which 186 tribal members gave up their 160-acre parcels in exchange for 186 10-acre allotments with fully irrigable water rights attached. These rights were to be served by the project, in perpetuity, at no cost to the tribe. Upon completion of the project, water sufficient to serve 1,860 acres was supplied to the tribe. Additional acreage was later added to the reservation, bringing the total to 5,400 acres, all with attached water rights. The water rights for these *additional* acres were never served, however (although the original water rights were).

That continued to be the case, in spite of the passage in 1978 of Public Law 95-337, which recognized the failure of the government to meet its contractual obligations to the tribes, increased the size of their reservation by an additional 2,700 acres, and mandated that the government act on its obligation to deliver water to the reservation. The law also directed the secretary of the interior to "reclaim the land and bring 1,800 acres into cultivation."[25] The mandate of the 1978 act was not carried out.

It was under these complex circumstances that a final attempt to negotiate and have approved an interstate compact between the states of Nevada and California occurred in the late 1980s.

Chapter Four

Coming to Terms

After the defeat of the Laxalt compact, it appeared that no additional efforts would be made to settle the water issues between California and Nevada, much less among the users in each state. Joe Gremban, president of Sierra Pacific Power Company, desperately needed an agreement that would enable Westpac, its water purveyor, to demonstrate that it would be able to deliver water to the Reno-Sparks area, under all conditions, to the estimated future population of the area. Otherwise, Westpac approval to continue operating might be withdrawn by the Public Service Commission. As described in the last chapter, Westpac's earlier attempt to acquire water from Stampede Reservoir had failed. The secretary of the interior was obligated to provide Stampede Reservoir water for the threatened and endangered species in Pyramid Lake, which took precedence over municipal, industrial, or other uses.

To demonstrate that it had enough water supplies for drought protection, SPPCO needed changes in how the river system was operated because the company's storage space on the system was inadequate. SPPCO would have to be involved in the negotiation of any future agreement because it had been awarded rights to certain flows by various decrees (for example, the Truckee River General Electric Decree, which was later incorporated into the Orr Ditch Decree). To move in this direction, SPPCO was willing to work with the tribe if necessary. Also eager to resume negotiations was Joe Ely, chair of the Pyramid Lake Paiute Tribe. He and the tribe had been sharply criticized in the local press for being instrumental in defeating the Laxalt compact. When Joe Ely returned to Reno, Gremban called him to arrange a meeting. The two met for coffee at the Continental Lodge in Reno. According to Gremban:

We talked about how long it had been taking, how many years it's been under litigation. We jointly concluded that the only way this thing could ever be resolved is to negotiate an agreement that all parties could live with. . . . The time was appropriate; it was perfect, because the people who had drafted the original compact [which Congress refused to ratify] were now retired. And so these were new faces, new people, who were coming on board with a new perspective. And so we agreed we would move forward and continue working on this until we were able to come up with a settlement.[1]

The Preliminary Settlement Agreement

SPPCO typically had sufficient water supplies in most years, even during periodic but short-lived drought, but it could not handle an extended drought. The solution was to store water in Stampede Reservoir in nondrought years. Reclamation holds the storage permit for Stampede Reservoir, allowing up to 126,000 acre-feet to be captured and stored in any given year.[2] But because Stampede has a lower priority than most of the other reservoirs on the system, its average yearly capture and storage does not exceed 50,000 a-f.[3]

The US Fish and Wildlife Service, working with Reclamation and the tribe, formulated annual flow targets at the mouth of the lake that were based on water availability and recovery objectives and strategies. Reclamation would then provide the flow targets to the federal water master, who controls releases from federal Truckee River reservoirs according to standard regulations for operating the river. From viewing the historical records and working with consultants, SPPCO determined that it would need to use the water for drought protection in the Reno-Sparks area once or twice in any ten-year period.

SPPCO and the tribe entered into the Preliminary Settlement Agreement (PSA), which would permit SPPCO to store reserves in Stampede. When there were normal or wet years, water above a specified base amount could be converted to "fish credit water" on

April 15. The fish credit water would be controlled by the Fish and Wildlife Service and the Pyramid Lake Paiute Tribe. This arrangement would persist, *even after* the cui-ui and Lahontan cutthroat trout were removed from the endangered and threatened species lists.

The subtle benefit was that it would override an antiquated provision of an existing decree. At the time the Floriston rates were established in 1915, the hydroelectric power plants on the Truckee were generating 90 percent of the power used in the Reno-Sparks area. By 1990 they were generating less than 0.5 percent. Yet the existing decree required Truckee water to be released year-round to generate electricity. This requirement created an inflexible operating system. Changes in the way the river was operated could not be made without considering Floriston rates.[4]

SPPCO, which could still request year-round flows for the generation of year-round electricity, agreed not to do so. Specifically, Title II, Section 1, of the PSA stipulates:

For purposes of this Agreement only, Sierra agrees to waive its rights to require releases or pass throughs of water from the Truckee River Reservoirs solely for the generation of hydroelectric power pursuant to the Truckee River General Electric Co. Decree and Claim Nos. 5, 6, 7, 8 and 9 of the Orr Ditch Decree. The water to which Sierra's rights are waived pursuant to this Section shall become Fishery Credit Water subject to the limitations set forth in Section 27 of Article III of this Agreement and shall be held in storage in the Truckee River Reservoirs and released for the sole use and benefit of the Pyramid Lake Fishery.

This agreement, in turn, encouraged new thinking about how to operate and manage the Truckee River and the Newlands Project. The PSA was a great benefit to Pyramid Lake as well, in that the tribe gained control over the timing of water entering the lake. Finally, this agreement created an alliance between SPPCO and the Pyramid Lake Paiute Tribe.

The PSA subsequently became the cornerstone of what eventually became Public Law 101-618. Ely and Gremban agreed to push for a new negotiated settlement that would permanently resolve the myriad water conflicts in northern Nevada, including the inter-state allocation of water between California and Nevada. Both were persuaded that if the system were to be managed differently, all the needs on the system could be met, at least most of the time. As news of the agreement spread, the parties to those conflicts became more willing to negotiate a new settlement—except, ultimately, the Truckee Carson Irrigation District.

The federal government had not been involved in the negotiation of the PSA, which was largely the work of two attorneys: Sue Oldham for SPPCO and Robert Pelcyger for the Pyramid Lake Tribe. Because this agreement dealt with the operation of a federal reservoir, the federal government inevitably became involved.

The Reid Compact

Harry Reid was elected to Paul Laxalt's Senate seat in 1986. Having represented Clark County as a congressman, Reid was just begin-ning to pay attention to the water conflicts in northern Nevada, which had become front-page news. The *Reno Gazette-Journal*'s edi-torial board called upon Senator-elect Reid to state how he would address the drought-caused fall in reservoir levels, since 1983 was the most recent year in which all the reservoirs were full. This water shortage prevented Reno from growing, which translated into a stagnant economy. The editorial board's sentiment was echoed by the Chamber of Commerce, business interests, and ordinary peo-ple. On the night that Reid was elected, a reporter asked him what was the most important issue facing his state, and Reid replied, "The water wars in northern Nevada."[5]

After the PSA was reached, Marcus Faust, lobbyist for Sierra Pacific, met with Reid and asked for his help. Reid asked why he would want to get involved in an issue where Paul Laxalt had failed. Faust replied that if they did succeed, Reid would have accomplished something that Laxalt, one of the most powerful men in Washing-ton in the late 1980s, had failed to do. Reid thought about that for a minute and replied, "Okay."[6]

Speaking about the negotiations that ensued, Pelcyger recalled that working with Laxalt had always been a one-way street. Laxalt did not listen; he issued ultimatums. Pelcyger contrasted the two men's styles: "When we would sit down and negotiate under the auspices of Laxalt or others, sppco or the State of Nevada, or whoever else, would say 'This is what we want.' And we [the tribe] would say, 'No.' And Laxalt, or more typically his person, would join with the others in trying to ram it down the tribe's throat. There was never any attempt to use his influence to really facilitate or broker an agreement. Reid, when he came in, completely changed the nature of the dialogue."[7] Reid encouraged discussion, thinking beyond the past, and, where necessary, compromise. Because of his influence, a real, constructive dialogue emerged, one that continues to this day.

Reid offered the services of his staff and sent Wayne Mehl, his legislative director, to facilitate the negotiations in Reno. Once in Reno, Mehl met with as many people as he could to come to an understanding of the system and its historical and present problems. He also began to conclude—as Ely and Gremban had earlier —that the key to making changes in the system lay in timing. Not all parties needed water at the same time. The farmers needed water in the spring and summer. sppco needed water in drought years. The Pyramid Lake Paiute Tribe needed water to preserve the lake's fish and, by extension, the viability of the lake itself. Nevada was still concerned that California would eventually lay claim to enough water to cause a shortage disaster just over the border. California wanted to protect what it thought was its fair share of water on the system. Both states really wanted certainty about the amount of water they would have in the future.

Mehl realized the necessity of initially involving only the four players who essentially had veto power over any agreement that might be reached: California, Nevada, the federal government, and the Pyramid Lake Paiute Tribe. He scheduled meetings among them early in the process to resolve any major differences. sppco was also included in the initial discussions because, although it did not have veto power, it was party to the PSA and wielded significant economic and political power at the time.

The process was helped by Reid's being in the majority party and on the Senate Appropriations Committee. He was also perceived by the Pyramid Lake Paiute Tribe as more supportive than Laxalt had been. Senator Reid sent a letter to the various parties encouraging them to participate in the new round of negotiations. Ultimately, Senator Reid's role was "invaluable in cajoling and pressuring and sometimes giving Dutch blessings to the tribe and in moving the process along to the point where an agreement was reached. Whenever—and it worked both ways—one party was becoming recalcitrant and it looked as though [the negotiations might] break down, the Senator would call and say 'I understand you're having a problem.' "[8] Once an agreement was reached, Reid steered it through Congress, helped along the way by colleagues in both houses and in key departments and agencies.

Thus, Reid had to navigate the conflict-laden waters on Capitol Hill, as well as the ideological and geopolitical conflicts in Nevada (Republican-Democrat, conservative-liberal, status quo–change, and rural-urban). Reid "had to really exercise an extraordinary amount of control over disparate interests who did not [always] see it in their interest to cooperate."[9]

Previous discussions had been marked by antagonism, which pitted the non-Indian interests against Indian claims. The Indians were pushed into the background. In contrast, the parties to the 1987 negotiations seemed ready (with the exception of TCID) to bargain, instead of going back to court.

The Fallon Paiute Shoshone Tribe was excluded from these discussions, because the tribe was negotiating a separate agreement with the federal government. Further, the legal position of the tribe was so strong that the federal government was already committed to remedying its situation.

TCID Withdraws

Although TCID initially took a seat at the negotiating table, its representatives seemed reluctant to engage fully. By June 1988, it withdrew from the negotiations. Pelcyger thought that TCID believed it had nothing to gain—and perhaps everything to lose—by participating and might stand a better chance of protecting its interests in the courts. Frank Dimick, western relations liaison for Reclamation at the time, mirrored this sentiment, noting that "TCID felt that there was nothing to bargain for; there [were] different perceptions regarding what happened on the day [TCID] walked out. They voluntarily left, but since there seemed nothing to gain, they were squeezed out. Why negotiate for less water? No one left them anything to bargain with, no chips on the table."[10] Gremban tried repeatedly to get TCID to stay in the negotiations, to no avail. He believes this is because TCID "represents a group of farmers [who are] independent and they feel that what they had was theirs and nobody should ever be able to take it away from them. And they honestly felt that this water was their water, and therefore the government shouldn't have anything to do or say [about] how it was going to be utilized."[11] Zell thought otherwise:

Well, [TCID was] from the very outset, from the very first time they ever appeared before the Senate committees, it was clear that they were going to be the intransigent players in this scenario. They continued to be hostile to the tribal efforts, what the tribe perceived as its interests. They saw their interests as being inimical to those of the tribe. They eventually stirred up an enormous backlash among non-Indian irrigators in the area, people who had not [previously] seen this to be a controversy in which they needed to involve themselves, so they ultimately became very politically active at the local level. But it was absolutely no surprise that they would ultimately drop out, because they were, as far back as I can recollect, sending shots across the various parties' bow that, "We're not going to come into this lightly, if at all. Don't take us for granted. Don't think that there's any deal that can be struck that isn't shaped around what our objectives and priorities are, and then we'll talk about what other people need."[12]

Despite the rejection of the process by TCID, negotiations continued through the spring of 1989. The early negotiations took the form of small meetings of select groups on issues of mutual concern. These groups worked together on one piece of an agreement at a time. Mehl helped write the appropriate language and kept the senator informed. The meetings were gradually expanded in summer 1989 to include the State of California, the US Fish and Wildlife Service, the Fallon Naval Air Base, the Cities of Reno and Sparks, Reclamation, and the Bureau of Indian Affairs. Reclamation, the Bureau of Indian Affairs, and the Fish and Wildlife Service needed to approve the agreement before Congress would ratify it. As the negotiations continued, it became increasingly clear that unless the settlement adequately addressed the legal and political problems facing the federal government regarding Indian tribes and the environment, approval by Congress would not be forthcoming.

After the more contentious elements of the agreement were worked out, sessions were held that included all interested parties. These included environmental groups advocating protection of the wetlands, most notably the Lahontan Valley Wetlands Coalition. The Wetlands Coalition embraced—and pushed—the idea of saving *both* Pyramid Lake and the wetlands in Lahontan Valley. Previously, the thinking was that it was a question of protecting either the fish or the wetlands but not both. These sessions provided participants the opportunity to report what had been accomplished to date and to obtain input from all.

Remarkably, an agreement was reached in less than two years. A draft of the Truckee-Carson–Pyramid Lake Water Rights Settlement Act was submitted to the Senate on August 4, 1989. Before discussing the provisions of Public Law 101-618, an examination of the way in which the bill moved through Congress provides interesting insights about the "black box" of Washington politics, which is covered in the following chapter.

Chapter Five

~~~~~~

Navigating Congressional Waters

Many observers at the time viewed Public Law 101-618 as a momentous achievement, especially given the number and scope of the conflicts involved. It not only would go far toward resolving northern Nevada's long-standing water problems, but could also serve as a model for resolving similar western water disputes. The bill would never have been passed, however, without the aid of key players in Congress and the federal bureaucracy.

According to Harry Reid, the support and leadership of Senator Bill Bradley were crucial to passage of the "negotiated settlement" (Public Law 101-618). Given Bradley's willingness to help defeat the Laxalt compact, it was no surprise that he was receptive to Reid's request for help. As chair of the Senate Subcommittee on Water and Power (of the Senate Energy and Natural Resources Committee), which had jurisdiction over the bill, Bradley became well versed in not only the provisions of the settlement but western reclamation policy as well. He questioned the continued support of western irrigation projects, especially given the increased competition for water from environmental, Native American, and urban interests. Other legislators noted that farmers in Maine were going bankrupt without federal water subsidies, while western farmers, living in the desert, were flourishing because of them. Senator Reid captured the essence of these views:

The Newlands Project is owned not only by the taxpayers of Nevada, but by the taxpayers of the country. In the growing West, we can no longer afford to squander the precious resource of water, nor can the federal government afford to provide subsidies in the form of artificially low water prices. In addition, the government must begin to scrutinize the use of water from federally owned facilities to accommodate a broader range of needs, including environmental restoration, as well as urban use. I believe that legitimate agricultural needs can be met, but they must be part of an overall picture, not the sole snapshot.

In addition to the support of legislators such as Bradley, approval was needed from key components of the Washington bureaucracy, many located in the Department of the Interior. Indeed, cooperation with Interior was vital for passage of the bill. Cooperation *within* the department was difficult to obtain, however.

For example, in February 1990 three Interior Department undersecretaries testified about the proposed compact before Bradley's subcommittee: John Sayre, assistant secretary for water and science; Constance Harriman, assistant secretary for fish and wildlife and parks; and Eddie F. Brown, assistant secretary for Indian affairs. All of them seemed unprepared, and their responses were inconsistent with each other. This seemed to astonish Bradley.

All three began their testimony by apologizing for not having submitted prepared statements by the deadline, not exactly an auspicious beginning. All three stated they could not support the bill unless their concerns were addressed, in very specific—and very different—ways. When questioned by Bradley, none of the representatives seemed as familiar with the issues surrounding the Newlands Project as Bradley expected them to be. "I do not know" was frequently the response to Bradley's numerous questions—apparently because of the "complexities" involved. The senator responded, "I understand. It is so complicated that for 50 years it has defied your best efforts. Let me ask you, all three of the Interior Department's divisions here received a consultant's report in, I think, August 1987 that detailed a wide variety of operational and structural changes that could be made in the Newlands project to increase efficiency and decrease water use. Are you familiar with that report?"[1]

None was aware of having received the report. Had they been, their positions and testimonies might have been very different. All three had insisted that operational and structural changes must be made before they could support the legislation, unaware that those changes had been recommended in the report. As is customary when the presidency changes hands—in this case, from Ronald Reagan to George Bush—top-level administrators in the executive branch were replaced. These replacements included the three under-secretaries who were giving testimony before Bradley's committee. John Sayre, a lawyer from Denver and completely unfamiliar with Newlands Project issues, seemed the most disadvantaged. This was his first congressional hearing. He relied on information given to him by Reclamation, which, "being the sponsoring agency that created the Truckee-Carson Irrigation District, had a natural sympathy to [the farmers'] position . . . [and, consequently, Sayre's presentation] totally reflected TCID's point of view, which at that point in time was simply not the politically popular thing to say in front of a Democratic Congress and committee chaired by Senator Bradley."[2] That three Interior representatives opposed the bill seemed to shock Bradley, who had anticipated a unified position in support of the bill.

Senator Bradley closed his session by stating the following: "Well, let me say that this is a less than satisfactory series of responses from the Department of the Interior on an issue area that involves most of the key problems facing the Bureau, the 'new' Bureau that is.[3] I had hoped that you would be able to be a little more forthcoming in trying to resolve these problems and, absolutely, in preparing for a hearing [such as this one]. Neither our guests nor I have heard that today, and I, for one, am less than pleased."[4] Reclamation's reputation was greatly damaged by its continued call for business as usual, which meant advocating the interests of the irrigators above all others.

Reid and Congresswoman Barbara Vucanovich contacted the secretary of the interior, Manuel Lujan, who subsequently ordered the formulation of an intradepartmental committee to iron out disagreements and produce a unified position. Members of this committee helped draft the amendment language that was eventually signed into law.

The Office of Management and Budget and the Senate Select Committee on Indian Affairs influenced a major component of the settlement, namely, the amount of money to be allocated to the Pyramid Lake Tribe. Although OMB insisted that the offer of sixty-five million dollars was too high, the Senate Select Committee thought the offer was fair, and the tribe was in agreement. Reid, although concerned that OMB's opposition might dissuade the president from accepting this section of the bill, decided to go with the committee's recommendation. The president did not protest.

A Second Chance?

By July 1990, Public Law 101-618 was ready to move out of committee and onto the Senate floor for debate. At that time, however, TCID seemed to finally realize that it was really being left out. TCID persuaded Senator Richard Bryan (D-NV) and Governor Bob Miller to request that Reid and Bradley postpone moving the bill through the Senate, giving TCID one last chance to cut a deal. Bryan and Miller were convinced they could persuade the tribe and TCID to meet and reach an agreement. Their basic point was, "This isn't really a settlement, because how can you have a settlement without TCID?" Thus, a last-ditch effort was made to bring TCID into the process.

That was not about to happen, as it turned out. TCID launched a campaign against the bill after it had been introduced, in spite of the fact that the bill did not affect TCID's interests. District farmers marched in protest from downtown Reno to Carson City. They hung Reid in effigy. They portrayed him as a villain. They testified against the bill. They stirred up local interests that had not previously viewed themselves as having a stake in the matter. Reid was skewered in the local papers.

Subsequently, Section 209 was added to the bill during the August recess. Reid initially blocked its inclusion because he believed that some parts would be perceived as punitive to TCID. He was eventually persuaded that it should be included, a change of heart perhaps hastened by TCID's surprising opposition to a bill that was essentially neutral to TCID.

Section 209 expanded the uses of project waters to include fish and wildlife, municipal and industrial water supplies, water quality, recreation, and any other purposes recognized as beneficial under state water law. The amendments also mandated recoupment of project waters that had been diverted by TCID above the amount to which it was entitled, estimated at more than one million acre-feet at the time. The secretary of the interior was given leverage to force TCID to improve the efficiency of its irrigation systems. For seven years, none of the parties could litigate under the Endangered Species Act, a provision meant to get the sides to "pry their fingers off each other's throats" for a while, to give the settlement a chance to work.[5] The Committee on Energy and Water added these amendments when it reviewed the proposed legislation. Both Bradley and, eventually, Reid approved the amendments.

TCID believed that Section 209 was added in retaliation for the protest campaign it mounted when the original bill was submitted to Congress. Bob Pelcyger agreed with TCID. For Pelcyger, "the moral of the story was that when you cross Senator Reid, when you march against him and hang him in effigy, especially after so many attempts were made to bring TCID into the process, when the initial bill was neutral to TCID, you do so at your own peril."[6]

Thomas Jensen, who helped draft this section, disagrees. The Senate Energy and Water Committee simply reached the conclusion that it would be best to deal with these issues in Public Law 101-618. In his view, no part of Section 209 can be fairly characterized as vindictive. Indeed, the provision barring litigation for seven years applied to all parties, not just TCID. He later observed that the burden of that provision fell on all of the parties, not just TCID. It kept everyone out of court. Jensen notes, as well, that they were all concerned that the tribe would continue to "just kick the living hell out of the farmers" and the whole deal would fall apart.[7]

Whatever the true motivation, it seems TCID missed a huge opportunity. According to Faust, this was one of many opportunities where TCID could have "cut a fat hog." They could have had "the newest, shiniest, brightest, most water efficient, sprinkled pivot irrigation water project in the Western United States," and it would not have cost them one penny.[8] The costs would have been repaid with o percent interest over fifty years from power revenues. All TCID had to do was come on board. It repeatedly refused to do so.

In Jensen's view, TCID continued to believe that it was going to keep getting 406,000 a-f-y like it always had. TCID also had a false sense of what the political reality was—its members still thought they could kill the bill.[9]

The Train Leaves the Station

Bradley and Reid became exasperated. They informed the parties that "this train is leaving the station. You get on it or you don't, but we're never going to revisit this [issue again]."[10] This same message was ultimately communicated to the Fallon Paiute Shoshone Tribe, whose separate negotiations with the federal government might have resulted in a protracted legislative battle as well. Reid, who was up for reelection in 1992, simply lacked the time or energy for another round like this one. Reid informed the Fallon tribe that if they were going to get their claims settled, it was going to have to be on the back of the Pyramid Lake settlement. Curiously, it turned out to be the reverse: the Pyramid Lake settlement wound up being appended to the Fallon Paiute Shoshone bill.

The Office of Management and Budget played a key if unintended role here by imposing strict guidelines regarding when water settlement negotiations "come to fruition . . . in legislative form and [are] brought to the Congress . . . because we are now entering times of budgetary constraints and . . . don't have the wherewithal to fund every settlement that might come to the fore."[11] When requested by the tribe to push through its settlement, the Department of the Interior, citing OMB's regulations, refused. At that point, Patricia Zell and the Senate Committee on Indian Affairs intervened and persuaded Interior to let a final settlement be developed and submitted in that legislative session. She described the process: "We had the tribe's wish list and we had what the Bureau of Reclamation felt was reasonable and we began, in the space of a week's time, hammering out a settlement, much to the chagrin of OMB. I must say there has never been a settlement that was put together and then put through the legislative process as quickly as the Fallon Paiute [Shoshone] settlement was. But those were the political realities and they could not be ignored."[12] The fact that the settlement language was drafted and the bill pushed through Congress in a week's time was nothing short of a miracle, especially given the two years it had taken them to reach this point.

Legislative Politics

The Pyramid Lake settlement bill, with the Fallon settlement appended to it, existed in two forms. One was attached to an omnibus water bill that became the subject of disagreement between the House and the Senate. The package was stalled by Senator Pete Wilson of California out of concern that certain provisions of the settlement would have disadvantaged Central Valley growers. Realizing that the omnibus bill was not going to make it out of the Senate, Reid tried to persuade the Department of the Interior to ask the Senate to pull out the Truckee-Carson Settlement bill and let it go through "without being held hostage to these other interests."[13] Interior gave no indication that it would do so.

Without consulting Bradley or others who were working to move the omnibus water bill, a frustrated Reid submitted the legislation to the Senate as a stand-alone bill. But instead of attaching the Fallon Paiute proposal to the Pyramid Lake proposal, he camouflaged the Pyramid Lake language by tacking it on to the Fallon Paiute bill. In this way, both bills would pass as one. Attention, if any was paid this late in the legislative process, would be focused on the relatively innocuous Fallon settlement rather than on the battle-scarred Pyramid Lake settlement. It was a legislative strategy that worked. As a result, the act moved quickly through review by the Senate Indian Affairs Committee, where it passed unanimously. The bill passed out of the Senate in the final days of the session.

It moved to the House on the last day of the session. In the closing hours of the 101st Congress, Reid persuaded the chair of the

Merchant Marine Fisheries Committee, Gary Studds, to waive the jurisdiction of his committee so that the bill could get through. Studds accommodated Reid's request. Public Law 101-618 was the second-to-last bill to pass that session. It was also the only water-related bill in a period of six years to be passed on its own.

According to Jensen, the bill slipped past everyone who had worked on it. Jensen saw it go on the floor and did not even recognize it. It took him nearly a half hour to realize what had happened. Reid was ecstatic.

I saw him immediately after the bill passed. It was two or three in the morning, and his office is in the Hart Building. My office was adjacent. . . . It was the second to last or last measure cleared by the House. We'd gotten it out of the Senate and were trying to get it out of the House before we adjourned for this session. It passed and I got up out of my office, walked around the corner . . . into that wonderful atrium of the Hart Building, and I saw Harry Reid, this normally very staid guy, bouncing out of his office doors, literally bounding . . . with his hands over his head going, "We did it! We did it!" He's all by himself. The lights were on in his office and staff members still in there, but he comes bouncing down the hallway outside of his office, and bounces out of the building just exalting the whole way. It was one of the most delightful scenes.[14]

Public Law 101-618 was signed into law by George H. W. Bush in November 1990.

Contributing Factors

One pivotal aspect of the process concerned the united front presented by the Nevada delegation. Senator Richard Bryan and Representatives Barbara Vucanovich and James Bilbray all favored the amended legislation. Had Vucanovich, a Republican and a longtime elected official in Nevada drawn from the Laxalt camp, wanted to do so, she could have killed the bill in the House.

There was also the fact that once Jensen became involved in the negotiations that led to Public Law 101-618, the nature of the discussions seemed to change. He persuaded the parties to focus on the long-term future of the watershed. According to Zell, Jensen "ultimately and skillfully used the power and authority of his principal, Senator Bradley, to, in some cases, foist upon the parties terms that they [might] not have introduced on their own." He held many meetings, both in DC and in Nevada, and spent an "extraordinary" amount of time educating people. He was a "great equalizer" as well, because he conveyed to the parties that, in the eyes of the Senate committee and Senator Bradley, none of them had a higher standing than any of the others. He asked them to consider seriously what was the right and responsible thing to do in this case.[15]

Another crucial aspect of the bill's passage was the united front of the local parties involved in the initial negotiations. Those that had veto power—Nevada, California, the federal government, and the Pyramid Lake Tribe—supported the measure. So did SPPCO, a powerful political player in its own right. TCID ultimately did not have enough influence to stop the negotiations or block passage of the bill.

According to Jensen, several threads were woven together to make this happen. There were some "very innovative dealmakers" involved, especially Ely and Gremban. SPPCO was "smart" and "innovative." Gremban realized that SPPCO no longer needed to ally with agricultural interests. If anything positive was going to happen, he had to work with the Pyramid Lake Paiute Tribe. There was also an "inquisitive and reform-oriented Senator," Bill Bradley. And then there was Senator Harry Reid, who "took a risk that no other western politician had ever done in the history of the country."[16]

The federal government seemed to be sending a signal to western states regarding the future direction of reclamation politics and policy in the United States: no more business as usual. In response to increasing disenchantment with (and criticism of) reclamation projects in general, and inefficient, uneconomical irrigated agriculture in particular, there was a growing consensus that the federal government should move in a new reclamation water policy direction. In the case of the Newlands Project and Public Law 101-618, that is exactly what happened. The provisions of this law are discussed in the following chapter.

The Carson River Diversion Dam is on the Carson River, approximately five miles below the Lahontan Dam. It is used to divert water into two main canals for irrigation of lands in the Carson Division of the Newlands Project. Courtesy U.S. Department of the Interior, Bureau of Reclamation.

The Lake Tahoe Dam is a concrete dam with seventeen vertical gates used to regulate water outflow into the Truckee River. Courtesy U.S. Department of the Interior, Bureau of Reclamation.

FACING PAGE:

Top: *Lahontan Dam and Reservoir is used to store and divert water to support agriculture in Lahontan Valley. Courtesy U.S. Department of the Interior, Bureau of Reclamation.*

Bottom: *Derby Dam captures Truckee River water and moves it into the diversion canal, where it travels to Lahontan Reservoir and, combined with water from the Carson River, supports agriculture along the canal and in the Newlands Project area in Lahontan Valley. Courtesy U.S. Department of the Interior, U.S. Bureau of Reclamation.*

Pyramid Lake is home to the Lahontan cutthroat trout and the cui-ui. Both fish have been declared endangered. A major goal of the negotiated settlement was to increase water supplies to the lake. Courtesy U.S. Department of the Interior, Bureau of Reclamation.

Chapter Six

An End in Sight?

Public Law 101-618 attempted to address numerous water-related problems in northern Nevada, both between California and Nevada and among users within Nevada. These are its major provisions.

Title I: The Fallon Paiute Shoshone Tribal Settlement Act

Title I resolved the seventy-year-old dispute between the Fallon Paiute Shoshone Tribe and the federal government. It created a forty-three-million-dollar settlement fund for the tribe, to be allocated over a six-year period beginning in 1992. Interest income from this fund would be used for tribal economic development; none of the principal can be expended. No more than 20 percent of the annual income could be distributed to tribal members.

In consultation with the secretary of the interior, the tribe was required to develop a plan for managing the annual income and to submit a plan for improvement of the irrigation works on the reservation. The tribe also had to release all claims against the federal government resulting from the latter's seventy-year failure to deliver water to the water-righted allotments on the reservation, including those made in two lawsuits (*Northern Paiute Nation v. United States* and *Pyramid Lake Paiute Tribe of Indians v. Lujan*).

To implement Title I, Congress appropriated forty-three million dollars for the Fallon Paiute Shoshone Settlement Fund. These funds were disbursed over a six-year period, from 1992 to 1997, and placed in interest-bearing deposits with the Treasury Department. Income from the fund continues to be used for tribal development. For example, the tribe constructed and now operates a travel center to supply goods to the local population and tourists, thereby providing income to the tribe and employment opportunities for tribal members.

The tribe has dismissed all of its claims against the federal government and has formally accepted the limits on water rights to be served by the Newlands Project.[1] Finally, the tribe agreed to cooperate in the development and implementation of a plan to improve the efficiency of the irrigation systems on the reservation that utilize project water. The Department of the Interior was directed to pay for the cost of delivering project water to the reservation. Section 103(E) noted that nothing "in this subsection is intended to affect the jurisdiction of the Tribes or the State of Nevada, if any, over the use and transfer of water rights within the Reservation or off the Reservation, or to create any express or implied Federal reserved water right." This last clause suggests that the federal government did not intend to pursue reserved water rights for the tribe. The tribe, in essence, gave up its right to pursue reserved water rights in the future, in exchange for the benefits granted to them in the legislation.

Title II: The Truckee-Carson–Pyramid Lake Water Rights Settlement Act

It should be noted that none of the provisions detailed in Title II will become "fully effective" until the US Justice Department declares that this law has been "fully implemented." This means, among other things, that TCID must drop the lawsuits it initiated, challenging key aspects of the settlement.

INTERSTATE ALLOCATIONS OF WATER

The purposes of Title II were numerous. The first addressed the interstate allocation of the Carson and Truckee Rivers and Lake Tahoe. In essence, approximately 90 percent of the Truckee River and 80 percent of the Carson River were allocated to Nevada, with the remainder allocated to California.

Regarding Lake Tahoe, the total "annual gross diversions for use within the Lake Tahoe basin from all natural sources, including groundwater, and under all water rights in the basin, shall not exceed 34,000 acre-feet per year" (Section 204[b][1]). Of that total, 23,000 acre-feet were allocated to California, with the remainder being allocated to Nevada.

The Pyramid Lake Paiute Tribe

The Pyramid Lake Tribe, in exchange for dropping claims against the federal government, would receive twenty-five million dollars for enhancement of the two fish species that lived in the lake, as well as an additional forty million dollars for tribal economic development. Interest on the Fisheries Fund was to be used only for the operation and maintenance of fish facilities at Pyramid Lake, including the development and implementation of a fish preservation plan developed by the tribe and approved by both the US Fish and Wildlife Service and the secretary of the interior.

Five eight-million-dollar payments were made to the Pyramid Lake Economic Fund, beginning in 1992. Both the principal and the interest from this fund would become available to the tribe to craft and implement, in consultation with the secretary of the interior, a plan to develop "long-term profit-making opportunities for the Pyramid Lake Tribe and its members, to create optimum employment opportunities for tribal members, and to establish a high quality recreation area at Pyramid Lake using the unique natural and cultural resources of the Pyramid Lake Indian Reservation" (Section 208[a][3][A]). Although the tribe has complete discretion to invest and manage the fund, none of the principal of the fund could be used to develop, finance, or operate any form of gaming or gambling, except as may be provided by the Indian Gaming Regulatory Act (PL 100-497).

Title II also stated that no disbursements shall be made from the Economic Development Fund until the tribe adopted an economic development plan; on March 17, the tribal council unanimously approved a resolution formally adopting a two-volume Pyramid Lake Economic Development Plan (PL 33-11). That plan was awarded the Outstanding Plan Award by the Nevada Chapter of the American

Planning Association at the 2011 DoBoer Awards for Excellence in Planning. On March 23, 2011, a copy of the approved plan was submitted to the federal government.

The tribe then petitioned Senator Harry Reid to amend Public Law 101-618 to allow the tribe to have access to the Pyramid Lake Paiute Economic Fund, which not only includes the originally appropriated forty million dollars but accrued interest of more than sixty-five million dollars.[2] Reid will not grant that access until all of the provisions of the negotiated settlement are fully implemented.

Section 207 addresses the Cui-ui and Lahontan Cutthroat Trout Recovery and Enhancement Program. It directs the Department of the Interior to update and implement plans for recovery of both species. The updated cui-ui recovery plan was approved May 15, 1992; the updated recovery plan for Lahontan cutthroat trout was approved on January 30, 1995. Both are being implemented.

As a reminder, LCT were plentiful in both Lake Tahoe and Pyramid Lake through the turn of the twentieth century. The Lake Tahoe cutthroat population collapsed in 1939, largely due to "overfishing, destruction of spawning habitat, and the introduction of non-native species."[3] The cutthroats disappeared from Pyramid Lake by 1944, primarily due to the construction of Derby Dam. The dam diverted much of the Truckee River's water (and sometimes all of it) to support agriculture in Churchill County. Since the natural terminus of the Truckee was Pyramid Lake, the lake level eventually dropped eighty feet. A delta formed between the lake and the Truckee River, preventing the fish from spawning. The LCT and the cui-ui were listed as threatened and endangered, respectively, in the 1970s. At the same time, assuming the original strain of the LCT population was gone completely, the Pyramid Lake Tribe began to raise a different strain of LCT from stocks outside the Truckee River Basin. The tribe has been restocking the lake with that strain of LCT ever since.

In the late 1970s, Bob Behnke, a taxonomist, collected trout from a small stream in the Pilot Peak Mountains on the Nevada-Utah border. He concluded that those fish were related to the original Pyramid Lake stock, which was confirmed decades later based on DNA tests. Indeed, Mary Peacock, professor of biology and an expert in genetics at the University of Nevada, Reno (UNR), asserted, "When you ask the question where these fish came from, the answer is very clearly from the Truckee River system—from Pyramid Lake."[4] The US Fish and Wildlife Service began raising the Pilot cutthroats in its Garnerville hatchery in 1995; the Pyramid Lake Tribe gave it permission to introduce the Pilot Peak cutthroat trout into Pyramid Lake, which they began to do in 2006.

In an amazing turnaround, only seven years later, fishermen were catching Pilot Peak cutthroats weighing seventeen to twenty-four pounds. According to Fred Crosby, owner of Crosby's lodge at Sutcliff, the news of the Pilot Peak cutthroats is gaining attention in fishing magazines and blogs around the country. He speculates that within three years, there will be Pilot Peak cutthroat trout in the lake that weigh thirty pounds or more. The largest LCT ever recorded weighed forty-one pounds. Crosby states that the long-term outlook for the Pyramid Lake fishery is very promising. Tribal planner Scott Carey agrees. The success of the Pilot Peak cutthroat bodes well for "conservation goals and the tribe's overall economy."[5]

Truckee River Operating Agreement

Section 205 required the Department of the Interior to negotiate a new operating regime for managing the Truckee River. Specifically, Section 205(a)(1) states: "The operating agreement will modify the existing method of river regulation in order to carry out the Preliminary Settlement Agreement . . . and will set forth criteria and procedures for the satisfaction of other water rights on the river system . . . [and] also provide for improved coordination of reservoirs to satisfy instream beneficial uses of water in the Truckee River, such as fish and wildlife habitat, recreation, and water quality."

This proved to be more arduous than negotiating Public Law 101-618. After more than seventeen years, the parties finally issued a draft Truckee River Operating Agreement on August 28, 2007. The required Environmental Impact Statement/Environmental Impact Report—jointly conducted by the Department of the Interior and the California Department of Resources—was issued in January 2008. An official signing was held in Reno on September 6, 2008. The required signatories included the States of California and Nevada, the Department of the Interior, the Truckee Meadows Water Authority, and the Pyramid Lake Paiute Tribe, the major players in the negotiation process.[6]

It seems that TROA was worth the wait. Essentially, the operation of five federal reservoirs[7] and two nonfederal reservoirs[8] was to be modified in order to "increase the operational flexibility and efficiency" of these reservoirs in order to provide "additional opportunities to store water in existing reservoirs for future municipal and industrial demands during periods of drought conditions in the Truckee Meadows, and enhance spawning flows to the lower Truckee River for the benefit of Pyramid Lake fishes."[9] Additionally, TROA would ensure that water is stored and released from Truckee River reservoirs to satisfy the terms of the Orr Ditch and Truckee River General Electric Decrees. It would also increase recreational opportunities in the federal reservoirs, improve stream flows and fish habitat throughout the Truckee River Basin, and improve water quality in the Truckee River.

Because the provisions of the Preliminary Settlement Agreement were incorporated into the law, the secretary of the interior entered into an agreement with SPPCO and the Pyramid Lake Tribe to store water owned by the power company in Stampede Reservoir, in order to provide water both for drought protection and for spawning of the Pyramid Lake fish. One of the most significant aspects of TROA is the creation of opportunities for storing and managing categories of "credit water." Once TROA goes into effect, the signatories will be permitted to accumulate credit water in reservoirs by capturing water that would otherwise have been released to serve a downstream water right. When credit water is accumulated, it could be retained in storage or *exchanged among the reservoirs* until needed to satisfy a beneficial use. According to the Environmental Impact Statement/Environmental Impact Report:

By providing operational flexibility in the exercise of existing water rights, TROA would allow opportunity to tailor reservoir operations to enhance specified resources. By not requiring construction of water storage and other facilities, TROA would not preclude implementation of technologically more advanced measures to provide additional water or improve water quality at some future time. TROA also would allow opportunity to enhance benefits for economic, social, biological, and trust resources in the study area, which previously had no water rights or had water rights of junior priority. Establishment of a habitat restoration fund could assist in restoring, enhancing, and protecting environmental values and processes long affected by more narrowly focused reservoir operations. As no significant adverse cumulative effects have been identified for the implementation of TROA, no mitigation would be necessary and none was recommended.

In order to become "effective," portions of TROA must be submitted to the US district courts that supervise and administer the Orr Ditch Decree and the Truckee River General Electric Decree for approval of any necessary modification that will need to be made to either. It also had to be promulgated as a federal regulation and published in the *Federal Register.*

TROA was promulgated as a federal regulation on December 5, 2008.[10] On November 17, 2008, the federal government filed a lawsuit to open the Orr Ditch Decree.[11] It has not yet filed a lawsuit to open the Truckee River General Electric Decree, although it plans to do so. Mary Conelly, Senator Reid's state director, expects that both courts will make the necessary adjustments to include relevant portions of TROA in the near future.

Environmental Impacts

Section 206 was intended to "ensure that the Stillwater marshes remain a viable migratory waterfowl wetland of at least 25,000 acres, even in drought years." Interior was authorized to purchase up to 75,000 a-f of water rights from willing sellers to meet the goals of this provision. The Lahontan Valley and Pyramid Lake Fish and Wildlife Fund was established, to be managed by the US Fish and Wildlife Service, on behalf of the Lahontan Valley wetlands and Pyramid Lake.

Through a partnership involving Nevada, the Nature Conservancy, the Nevada Waterfowl Association, the Bureau of Indian Affairs, and Reclamation, 34,000 a-f of water has been purchased from the Carson Division of the Newlands Project to sustain the Lahontan Valley wetlands. In addition, the US Fish and Wildlife Service purchased 4,300 a-f of water from the Carson River. It received an additional 2,900 a-f from the Fallon Naval Air Station, for a total of 41,800 a-f. These water rights were purchased from willing sellers at appraised market value. Most purchases in the Carson Division occurred at the edges of the Newlands Project, near Stillwater Wildlife National Refuge and Carson Lake. However, water cannot be purchased for the Lahontan Valley wetlands from the Truckee Division of the Newlands Project. To deliver these water supplies to Stillwater, the secretary of the interior is permitted to use federal facilities (dams, reservoirs, ditches) and to pay TCID for the costs of delivery. To achieve this goal, a contract was negotiated between Reclamation and TCID, which was signed on November 26, 1996, with an effective date of January 1, 1997.[12] The contract will remain in effect for twenty-five years, with possible five-year extensions after expiration. Stillwater National Wildlife Refuge now encompasses 77,520 acres. The entire Stillwater National Wildlife Refuge Complex consists of Stillwater Refuge, Fallon Refuge, and Anaho Island Refuge, altogether constituting 163,000 acres of wetland and upland habitat.

Section 219(b)(2) transfers Anaho Island to the Pyramid Lake Reservation and orders that it be held in trust by the US government for the tribe with administration by the Fish and Wildlife Service "as an integral component of the National Wildlife Refuge system for the benefit and protection of the colonial nesting species and other migratory birds."

In a separate but related event, in the late 1980s the Pyramid Lake Paiute Tribe sued the Environmental Protection Agency over the quality of the lower Truckee River water. Codefendants included the Cities of Reno and Sparks, Washoe County, the Department of the Interior, the Department of Justice, and the Nevada Division of Environmental Protection. In an effort to settle out of court, the parties sought a negotiated resolution to the problem. The end result was the Truckee River Water Quality Agreement (wqa), signed by all parties on October 10, 1996.

Under this agreement, Reno and Sparks and Washoe County agreed to spend twelve million dollars, with matching funds provided by the federal government, for the purchase of water rights for the sole purpose of improving water quality in the river. The plan was to use the water to dilute the discharge from the Reno-Sparks wastewater treatment facility and other sources in order to meet national water-quality standards. The water will be stored in federally owned reservoirs upstream and released as required. In exchange, the tribe agreed to drop the lawsuit. Thus far, the parties have acquired more than 7,000 a-f of Truckee River water rights, "in perpetuity," under the wqa.

These three entities later agreed to provide an additional 6,700 a-f of water to further improve the water quality of the Truckee River, the amount estimated to be available from water underlying city and county streets. It turned out that this was an overestimation. To date, they have acquired 3,500, leaving them with a balance of 3,200 a-f. Given today's water market, they are unable to afford the cost of purchasing an additional 3,200 a-f of water. The parties are working with the federal government to obtain funding to purchase 3,200 a-f of water.

The idea is to enhance the water quality of the Truckee River before it flows into Pyramid Lake, in order to accomplish a number of goals, most notably preservation of the lct and cui-ui and conservation and restoration of the river and lake ecosystems.

The Newlands Project

Section 209 of Public Law 101-618 concerns the Newlands Project and TCID. Reid initially blocked this from being included in the bill. After TCID staged protests in Reno, and under pressure from Senator Bradley and other eastern senators, he relented—and Section 209 was added. First, the legal purposes that Newlands Project water could serve were expanded to include fish and wildlife, municipal and industrial water supplies, water quality, recreation, and any other purposes recognized as beneficial under state water law. Moreover, these purposes must be met in a manner that would not increase diversions from the Truckee River beyond those currently allowed or conflict with applicable court decrees.

The Department of the Interior was authorized to undertake a study to increase project efficiency[13] from 45 to 75 percent, consider the impact of increased efficiency on groundwater supplies and on the wetlands in Churchill County, enter into agreements to allow water rights holders to use Newlands Project facilities for storage of water for drought protection, and undertake recreation and effluent-reuse studies. Section 209(i) mandates that the Department of the Interior, "insofar as is consistent with project irrigation purposes and applicable operating criteria and procedures," manage Newlands Project reservoirs for the benefit of fish and wildlife.

Section 209 also authorized the study of water banking, recreational uses of project facilities, reuse of effluent, and cancellation of repayment obligations to Reclamation by TCID. None of these may be undertaken, however, until TCID has "entered into a settlement agreement with the Secretary concerning claims for recoupment of water diverted in excess of the amounts permitted by applicable operating criteria and procedures" (Section 209[h][1]).

The recoupment issue centers on the claim by the Pyramid Lake Tribe that from 1973 to 1988, TCID diverted more than 1 million a-f of water from the Truckee River than it was entitled to divert. Hearings commenced in the US District Court for the District of Nevada. In 2003 the court decided that TCID was responsible for only 25 percent of the water it had overdiverted from 1973 to 1988 and ordered repayment of 197,152 a-f of water. Both TCID and the Pyramid Lake Paiute Tribe were dissatisfied with that amount and filed lawsuits.[14] The US District Court for the District of Nevada rendered its decision on October 6, 2011: TCID had to repay 309,480 a-f of the water that it had overallocated. Both parties have appealed the case to the US Court of Appeals for the Ninth Circuit. However, irrespective of the outcome of that case, TCID would take so long to pay back either quantity that doing so would have negligible effect on Pyramid Lake, especially in light of the ongoing drought.

The negotiated settlement stipulated that "all actions taken heretofore by the Secretary under any operating criteria and procedures [were] . . . declared to be valid and . . . not be subject to revision in any judicial or administrative proceeding" (Section 209[j][2]).

And finally, Section 210(a)(3) asserts that "no person or entity who has entered into the Preliminary Settlement Agreement as modified by the Ratification Agreement or the Operating Agreement, or accepted any benefits or payments under this legislation . . . may assert in any judicial or administrative proceeding a claim that is inconsistent with the allocations provided in Section 204 of this title, or inconsistent . . . with the operational criteria for the Truckee River established pursuant to Section 205 of this title." This section goes on to assert that no "person or entity who does not become a party to the Preliminary Settlement Agreement . . . or the Operating Agreement may assert in any judicial or administrative proceeding any claim for water or water rights for the Pyramid Lake Indian Reservation, or the Pyramid Lake Fishery. Any such claims are hereby barred and extinguished and no court of the United States may hear or consider any such claims by such persons or entities." Section 210(b)(10) noted that "nothing in this title shall be construed to create an express or implied Federal reserved water right." Thus, the Pyramid Lake Paiute Tribe forfeited any additional claims to reserved water rights by accepting the benefits provided to it by the settlement.

What happens while Public Law 101-618 continues to be implemented, TROA awaits court approval, the four lawsuits in which TCID is involved are finally resolved, and Reno, Sparks, and Washoe County meet their obligation to deliver an additional 3,200 a-f of water to the Truckee River remains to be seen. Currently, the parties are adhering to the terms of the negotiated settlement and TROA as if it were "fully effective."

Chapter Seven

Staying the Course

The fact that the agreement that became Public Law 101-618 was negotiated in only two years is astonishing, given the more than one hundred years of conflict, the seemingly endless litigation, the hostilities that existed, and the public nature of the entire process. Many factors contributed to "staying the course" during those negotiations.

One of these was what Wayne Mehl called "firm patience." One cannot hurry the process along—the parties balk when that happens. It is a lot like trying to "push a worm." It simply does not work.[1] The parties had to be given the time to reach conclusions themselves, and a facilitator has to let that happen. As Mehl noted, the tendency is to want to leap to the conclusion. There were times when he knew where the negotiation was headed on a given issue, but he let the parties work it out among themselves. They had to "own" the final decision, even if it took weeks to make it. Whenever too much pressure was applied, the group would start to lose its cohesiveness. Parameters needed to be set, to be sure. For any given meeting, the issues for discussion had to be identified and ancillary matters set aside. For each piece of the puzzle solved, the sunken costs became higher, providing additional incentives for everyone to remain at the table.

Another factor was the presence of at least one member of Congress who could persuade colleagues in both houses to approve the ultimate agreement. In this case, there were two: Senators Harry Reid and Bill Bradley.

Reid, then junior senator from Nevada, was the consummate politician here. He obtained the money to begin and sustain the negotiations. He sent one of his most skilled staffers, Wayne Mehl, to Reno to facilitate the negotiations. He stayed informed. He personally intervened when the negotiations seemed on the verge of falling apart. He helped move the bill through both houses of Congress, exhibiting a mastery of the legislative process.

Few freshman senators have the contacts, the knowledge, and the subtlety needed to get a major bill passed. Recall the words of Thomas Jensen: Reid "took a risk that no other western politician had ever done in the history of the country." Furthermore, Reid was the first western politician to understand that agricultural interests had grown less powerful. Jensen noted that Reid came to understand that the political dynamic had changed to the point where change was not only possible but imminent. He worked the system to help make that happen—and it was a very "gutsy" move. Western senators seldom cross agricultural water interests because they are powerful and entrenched—and can greatly influence election outcomes. Crossing that line will happen more as time goes on, as there are at least sixty other interstate disputes presently "raging in the West."[2]

The negotiated settlement also would never have become law without the leadership of Bradley. He opposed the Laxalt compact and was willing to debate Laxalt on the Senate floor if it had come for a vote. He provided enthusiastic support of the Reid proposal. He was chair of the Senate Subcommittee on Water and Power, which had jurisdiction over the bill. Prior to holding hearings, he immersed himself in the historical and contemporary conflicts surrounding the Newlands Project. When three divisions of the Department of the Interior failed to present a unified position on the bill, Bradley insisted that they develop one. Ultimately, that position was in support of the bill.

When the bill was reported out of the subcommittee, he vigorously lobbied colleagues to pass the omnibus water bill, to which the settlement was attached. According to Zell, "Senator Bill Bradley . . . was one who became integrally involved in all of the deliberations, and played a prominent role which ordinarily you wouldn't expect [on an issue like this] from a senator from New Jersey. Indeed, the ultimate settlement was very much shaped by his views and his plans for the overall watershed."[3]

Congresswoman Barbara Vucanovich was critical to passage in the House, even though killing the bill would undoubtedly have pleased her own rural constituents. She also advised TCID and the farmers it represented that she would not support any changes to the law. She was "steadfast" in her support of a bill she believed was an overall benefit to northern Nevada.

Another aspect was the formation of political alliances between parties that had been adversarial. When the Laxalt compact failed to pass, the Sierra Pacific Power Company and the Pyramid Lake Paiute Tribe realized they *had* to work together to resolve their respective problems. They entered into an agreement that broke the stranglehold that the Floriston rates requirement had on the operation of the Truckee River system. Their Preliminary Settlement Agreement became the backbone of Public Law 101-618 and the Truckee River Operating Agreement.

Additionally, the prior stance on fish and wetlands was that it was an either-or situation: if one could be saved, it would have to be at the expense of the other. The groups supporting protection of the wetlands and those supporting "saving" the LCT and cui-ui eventually realized that both could be protected—and vigorously pursued that outcome. These early alliances demonstrated that past animosities *could* be set aside. They also offered hope to other participants that an agreement that would be acceptable to Congress was possible—that common ground could be found. Thomas Jensen played a critical role here, because he was able to get the parties to think outside the historical box, focus on the long term, and consider the greater good.

Virtually everyone involved in the development of the negotiated settlement agreed that the real story was that of the Pyramid Lake Paiute Tribe—and its young leader, Joe Ely, who was only twenty-five years old when he defeated the Laxalt compact. Not only was Joe a young man, but he had absolutely no experience in congressional politics. Neither did tribal attorney Bob Pelcyger, who was accustomed to being in court. Together, they learned to successfully navigate the legislative process. Ely became a skilled poker player in a high-stakes game—and he played the game to the end in spite of the cards that were initially stacked against him.

There were hundreds of other players in this process by the time both the negotiated settlement and TROA were completed. Many of these people will remain involved as TROA continues to be implemented. But can this settlement be considered "successful"?

A Successful Settlement?

Five major criteria for defining settlement success have been overwhelmingly accepted by scholars. Is the agreement "fair"? Are the parties satisfied with the outcome? Has it resulted in better relationships? Have the skills and understanding of the parties improved? Will they be able to "more broadly cooperate" in the future? The answers to all of these questions appear to be yes, with some qualifications, especially with regard to TCID.

As is the case with most negotiations, not all parties received everything they wanted. It does appear that all of the parties *are* satisfied with the *overall* outcomes, though. The state and local interests that were involved (TCID aside) managed to obtain at least part—if not most—of what they wanted. Sierra Pacific wanted drought protection; it secured it for at least forty years. California and Nevada wanted assurance that a certain portion of the Truckee and Carson Rivers would be permanently allocated to each of them; they both received such assurance. The Pyramid Lake Tribe wanted sufficient money and water to maintain and enhance Pyramid Lake and its fisheries; it received some of both, and even if those amounts turn out to be insufficient in the long run, the agreement will have continued the trend of decisions favorable to the tribe and the lake. The Fallon Paiute Shoshone Tribe wanted compensation for the federal government's failure to carry out its obligations to them; the settlement provided forty-three million dollars in compensation. The environment is benefiting as well, because the settlement included provisions for the enhancement and maintenance of the wetlands and wildlife at the Stillwater National Wildlife Refuge.

The federal government might have benefited most of all. It was able to disentangle itself from the lawsuits to which it was still a party at the beginning of the negotiations. The federal government also recognized the environmental damage caused by the Newlands Project and moved to correct it, thereby enhancing its image in the environmental community.

The federal government ultimately had to acknowledge that reclamation policy had not yet caught up with its changed mission, one that requires it to embrace additional values and interests: environmental, recreation, fish and wildlife, Native American, and urban. As more employees of Reclamation who have the "old" mind-set retire, Reclamation will more completely become the "new" Reclamation to which Bradley referred in hearings on the settlement.

Asked if he thought the negotiated settlement was a good one, Ely responded:

I think it's a good deal. I think it's one of the better deals that I've seen out there, not only for us but for the other parties as well. I think one of the critical elements of a negotiated settlement is that it endures, and it doesn't endure if there are disgruntled parties. Litigation is the place for deceit, deception, and treachery. Not in a settlement. In a settlement, you have to have good faith. You have to go forward. You have to lay your cards on the table. You have to be a little bit vulnerable. And you have to say, "Now, if we put all these pieces together, what kind of puzzle do we come up with?" And then agree upon it and work it out. And you have to realize that there's compromise, and that people have to be happy with it. The states have to be happy with it. All the elements . . . Reno and Sparks and Sierra Pacific . . . they have to be happy with this particular piece, because if they're not, it'll unwind. At some point, it'll unwind. We always approached it from that standpoint. We weren't trying to nail anybody in this. I don't know of anybody who's gone through the settlement who is now unhappy with it. I think the only [entity that] wasn't happy was TCID, but they're not part of that agreement. I don't think they'll ever be happy.[4]

This sentiment has been echoed by Joe Gremban, Marcus Faust, Wayne Mehl, Thomas Jensen, and Sue Oldham,[5] as well as major political players in Washington, DC. Reid, Bradley, and Zell also indicated that this is a "model" settlement. Zell noted that the fact that this settlement continues to have such prominence in the universe of Indian water settlements suggests that it was a good settlement.

Among all the parties to the settlement, some lifelong friendships were formed. But all parties seemed to at least come to understand—and eventually respect—the other points of view. This spurs confidence that the parties will opt to address any new issues through bargaining rather than in the courts.

Unfortunately, TCID has continued litigating. It initiated a lawsuit against the Truckee Meadows Water Authority over the use of water stored in Donner Lake. It is party to the lawsuit over the recoupment issue. It has challenged various provisions of TROA, arguing, essentially, that the government has "failed to establish that the proposed changes will not injure existing water users, and Newlands Project water rights will in fact be injured."[6]

This is potentially tragic for all parties: the major provisions of the negotiated settlement and TROA will not be fully effective until all of the lawsuits related to both have been resolved. TCID's actions are puzzling, especially considering that TROA does not trump state law; its 1902 irrigation rights have not been taken away.

On a more positive note, beginning in the summer of 2012, TCID and the Pyramid Lake Paiute Tribe have been engaged in discussions that might lead to a resolution of the remaining conflicts. Indeed, an excerpt of TCID's August 7, 2012, board meeting minutes is quite revealing: "There are more commonalities than there are differences; children, farmers, agriculture and communities that need water to survive and sustain for the future. . . . We are all now in a place to stop fighting the ongoing war and spend time coming to an agreement with both the Tribe and TCID bringing to the table what they can for the future. We both have the same regional water issues impacting water users."

Perhaps TCID's newfound willingness to work with the tribe might be partially attributable to its dire financial condition. It has spent untold millions on lawsuits during the past fifty years, yet it has not fulfilled all of its operating and maintenance responsibilities on the system. A serious breach in the Truckee Canal occurred on January 5, 2008, flooding nearly six hundred homes in nearby Fernley. A class-action lawsuit has been filed against TCID. If the home owners win, TCID could be liable for fifteen to twenty million dollars in damages.

The Pyramid Lake Paiute Tribe also has a compelling interest in reaching an agreement with TCID, which would permit the tribe to access its forty-million-dollar Economic Development Fund, as well as the more than sixty-five million dollars that the fund has generated in interest.

If the parties can come to an agreement over the remaining issues between them—and TCID drops its lawsuits—Reid is committed to helping them implement the terms of whatever agreement they reach. Reid is quite clear, however: the two parties must work together to develop an agreement themselves. Mary Conelly, Reid's state director, is optimistic that this will occur in the near future. When that happens, the one holdup to full implementation of the negotiated settlement is the inability of Reno, Sparks, and Washoe County to deliver an additional 3,200 a-f to the Truckee River.

TCID—and Irrigated Agriculture in the West

Observers speculated as early as 1989 that Public Law 101-618 was the beginning of the end of the Newlands Project, a conclusion that others have since reached. Pelcyger has stated that "the writing is on the wall, that that project is doomed. It is just a matter of time." TCID and the Newlands Project farmers now stand alone; through the course of the negotiations, TCID and the other four major players became adversaries. As future issues arise, and they always do, the lineup might continue to be four to one. According to Pelcyger:

So the result of the legislation, one way of looking at the legislation, I think particularly significant . . . is that it was, in a way—we will see what happens—it was the first termination of a federal Reclamation project. Newlands was the first reclamation project. It resulted in the near destruction of two major ecosystems: Pyramid Lake and the Lahontan Valley wetlands. And now Congress has come along and basically provided for the eventual, I think, termination of the project by providing for the water rights . . . to be acquired, for the water to be redirected back to their original ecosystems. It takes about 125,000 a-f to service 25,000 acres of wetlands. The negotiated settlement directs the Secretary of the Interior to develop and implement the cui-ui recovery plan and that plan, developed and approved in 1992, calls for an additional 100,000 a-f of Truckee River water to flow to Pyramid Lake in order to achieve recovery, [and this is] over and above what Pyramid Lake is already receiving under the . . . OCAP [provisions]. Under this scenario, the acreage served by the Newlands Project may be reduced to 20,000 acres over time, which, coincidentally, was what the Carson River was supporting prior to Newlands.[7]

If this is the beginning of the end of the Newlands Project as we know it, an eventuality that Mehl seemed to lament, he believes that TCID bears much of the responsibility. TCID rejected numerous invitations to rejoin the negotiations, which were offered until just before the August recess in 1990. There were also chances for TCID to obtain benefits for the farmers and the community.

For example, in 1993, a second round of negotiations was initiated by the parties that had been negotiating Public Law 101-618. It was led by Gail Bingham, a renowned expert in natural resource conflict resolution. A major purpose of these negotiations was to prompt TCID to help address such issues as operating criteria for the Truckee River and recoupment. The parties were prepared to give TCID additional incentives to become involved, including a water treatment plant to address Fallon's drinking water problems. TCID's role was primarily that of an observer. The farmers were represented by the Lahontan Valley Environmental Alliance, a broad-based community group interested in the outcome.

Conelly attended these negotiations as part of a team of federal representatives. These representatives did not facilitate or actively engage in the negotiations. They were there primarily as observers and to convey the federal government's position on any potential outcome of the negotiations. Conelly observed that during these negotiations, the farmers' representatives seemed to oppose *any* alternatives that included benefits to the Pyramid Lake Tribe, regardless of the benefits that might have also accrued to the farmers or the other parties. These negotiations lasted nine months and ended in stalemate.

The way things worked out, Mehl has asserted, the Newlands Project could wind up being squeezed—and squeezed some more. For example, the federal government might increase the efficiency requirement for the project, or it might gradually reduce the amount of water diverted from the Truckee River. The Pyramid Lake Tribe has acknowledged that its long-term goal is to prevent *any* diversion of Truckee River water to Lahontan Reservoir. Had TCID stayed in the game, it could at least have been more certain of where it stood, now and in the future.

Lyman McConnell both agreed and disagreed with this assessment. It is true that TCID's relationship with Reclamation has changed dramatically. In his view, Reclamation has become, as the major agency responsible for implementation of 101-618, a "rule-enforcing watchdog." Some people in that agency still support irrigated agriculture and see themselves as responsible for its interests above all others. Such support has waned and will continue to do so. Once the generation of employees operating under the previous orientation retires, the Bureau of Reclamation will more completely embrace the changes that have been forced upon it. Nevertheless, he remains optimistic about the future of TCID, the Newlands Project, and irrigated agriculture in Churchill and Lyon Counties. Changes, when they come, are more likely to be a function of shifting demographics. Farmers will eventually retire and find that their children do not want to take their place. Increasing numbers of "hobby farmers" will move to the community—farmers whose operations are five acres or less. The area will continue to urbanize. These changes will be gradual, and the community will absorb those changes gradually as well.[8]

McConnell's assessment seems the most correct. After all, the Newlands Project continues to provide water to approximately fifty-five thousand acres of farmland in Lahontan Valley, near Fallon. The negotiated settlement, and the implementation of its various provisions, appears not to have disrupted the rural lifestyle enjoyed by residents in Churchill and Lyon Counties.

David Overvold, former manager of the Special Studies Division for the Bureau of Reclamation in the Lahontan Basin Area Office in Carson City, believes the change in the orientation of Reclamation is wrongheaded. He left the agency in 1997 and was project manager for TCID until October 2009. In his view, Reclamation was created to work with irrigation districts to serve the interests of western farmers. Instead, the farmers have been betrayed. The lawsuits and negotiations that led to Public Law 101-618, and the law itself, represent one "taking" after another. There was never anything to be gained by TCID's participating in the negotiations. He recalled that the question posed to TCID throughout this process was "What can *you* [TCID] do for *us* [the other parties]?" It was never "What can *we* do for *you*?"

Interestingly, TCID and four of its employees (David Overvold, Lyman McConnell, John Baker, and Shelby Cecil) were named in a ten-count federal indictment handed down in December 2008.[9] The indictment accused them of conspiracy to defraud the US Bureau of Reclamation, falsification of records, false claims, and false statements. According to the indictment, they allegedly inflated project efficiency data from 2000 to 2005 as part of a scheme to secure additional water supplies for Nevada farmers and ranchers—and to artificially reduce the water debt they owed to the Pyramid Lake Tribe. They were scheduled for trial in January 2010. Surprisingly, however, attorneys for the federal government and TCID reached an agreement in October 2009 to dismiss the charges against TCID, McConnell, and Baker. The indictment against Overvold was suspended for eighteen months. If he remained a "law-abiding citizen" during that period, the indictment against him would be dismissed. As part of that agreement, Overvold resigned from his job with TCID and agreed not to seek reemployment with the district.[10] Overvold abided by the terms of the agreement and is no longer under indictment.

Native Americans: The Two Tribes

In negotiated settlements that involve Native American tribes, an ongoing concern is whether the tribes will get their due. In practical terms, Native Americans cannot receive a truly just share of western water, because too much water has already been allocated. But can settlements provide an "approximation of justice in an imperfect world"?[11] In this settlement, I believe the answer is yes. The Fallon Paiute Shoshone Tribe not only received a forty-three-million-dollar compensation package but received "wet" water, to be served by the Newlands Project in perpetuity. It is true that both tribes gave up future reserved rights claims. But such claims would have been tenuous, given the current judicial climate, where the courts have been eroding the Winters Doctrine, limiting its applicability.

The Pyramid Lake Paiute Tribe benefited tremendously, in ways not anticipated at the beginning of this process. First, not only did it get a seat at the bargaining table, but its representatives in the negotiations assumed leadership roles. The tribe is now a major political player. Its compensation package included twenty-five million dollars for protecting and managing the lake's fish, as well as forty million dollars for economic development. Since the Economic Development Fund was created, it has generated more than sixty-five million dollars in interest. The tribe cannot access the latter two sources of money until TCID settles the lawsuits that it initiated after the negotiated settlement became law.

In retrospect, why TROA took more than seventeen years to complete is not fully explained by the law's not specifying a timeline or deadline. One cause is the lack of a shared vision for how TROA should provide for the operation of the Truckee River system to meet several broad goals. As a result, many battles, large and small, had to be fought to shape that vision. In addition to the five required signatories of TROA, many organizations, agencies, and levels of government were involved. As time went by, representatives of those groups changed, as did presidential administrations. This made sustained cohesion difficult. The parties to TROA had to find ways to overcome roadblocks, learn how to work together, develop mutual trust, and, most of all, figure out how to build flexibility into the system such that as many interests as possible could be served over time. The fact that an agreement was reached at all is a testament to their commitment and determination.

Concluding Observations

Native American water rights settlements involve different histories, contexts, power relationships, and, ultimately, outcomes. Nonetheless, some valuable lessons can be learned here that may be applied to future natural resource negotiations.

Past animosities must be put aside, so that trust can begin to be built among the parties. Keeping the initial negotiations small was helpful in this particular case; had all of the potential players been involved from the beginning, probably nothing would have been accomplished. Sunken costs are important. As each piece of what became the final agreement was reached, that piece was shaped by what had come before and also shaped what came after. Sunken costs are accumulated, making it more likely that the players will stay at the bargaining table.

A skilled facilitator—one who is committed to seeing the process through to the end—is also critical. Historically weaker players can benefit from the help of attorneys and lobbyists who understand how to identify and influence the key legislators and agencies at various levels of government.

Leadership is also critical to achieving agreement in the midst of protracted conflicts such as this. A certain kind of leadership was at play here: the emergent leader who, finding himself in a situation that requires leadership, rises to the occasion. Such leaders tend to be ambivalent—or even reluctant—at first. Senator Harry Reid was a freshman senator from Searchlight, Nevada, who did not realize, at the time, the weight of the task he had agreed to shoulder. Once thrust into a leadership position, he set aside his reservations and became deeply and passionately involved. Joe Ely was twenty-five years old, high school educated, a Native American, and a DC outsider. Determined that his tribe would not have the Laxalt compact forced upon them, he too became deeply and passionately involved. These two men tended to greet each new obstacle with more determination. Each of them seemed to regard failure as simply not an option. Although much credit can be given to the many people who worked on this law, those who participated in or observed the process that led to 101-618 spoke highly of the remarkable leadership—unexpected and maverick—displayed by Reid and Ely.

As Reid noted, Public Law 101-618 is now the law of the land. The overall benefit of the settlement is going to be measured in terms of generations, not years. The parties (TCID aside) found a way to yes. Five years down the road, they appear to have found ways to stay there.

Focusing on Walker Lake

The passage of PL 101-618 authorized the negotiated settlement of more than one hundred years of water resource conflicts in the Carson and Truckee Basins. Some of the content of and history behind that law might be relevant to similar issues in Walker Basin. Both Walker and Pyramid Lakes are desert terminus lakes and have experienced decreased inflows. Conflicts in both basins have involved agricultural users, Native American tribes, and environmentalists. A 1993 mediated attempt to resolve those conflicts in the Walker Basin failed. Unlike the Carson and Truckee Basins, in which the Newlands Project was constructed by the federal government, the irrigation system in Walker Basin was privately developed. There has been, therefore, no long-term historical involvement of the federal government in Walker Basin. Unlike Pyramid Lake, Walker Lake contains no endangered species.

The viability of Walker Lake has been threatened due to a significant increase in salinity, which is attributable to several factors. First, Walker Lake is overappropriated to agricultural interests in Smith and Mason Valleys, which translates into less and less water going to Walker Lake; by 1966 the lake level had dropped 108 feet since it was first measured in 1882. As of 2007, it had dropped 145 feet. Second, northern Nevada has experienced drought conditions off and on since the late 1980s; indeed, the worst period of drought in Nevada occurred in 1987–94. Increased salinity is also the result of the lake's natural geological feature: a layer of salt at the bottom of the lake. Other causes include industrial discharge, sewage, fertilizer and pesticides, road runoff, and soil erosion.

In 1992, under the provisions of the Western Water Policy Act of 1992 (PL 102-575), Congress directed the president to "undertake a comprehensive review of federal activities in the nineteen western states which directly or indirectly affect the allocation and use of water resources—whether surface or subsurface—and to submit a report of the findings and recommendations to the congressional committees having jurisdiction over federal water programs." The report noted that because at least fourteen federal agencies are involved in water policy, the result has been "unclear goals and an inefficient handling of the Nation's water policy . . . [and that] the conflicts between competing goals and objectives of federal, state, and local agencies and private users are particularly acute" in the West, in spite of the water policy "revolution" that began several decades ago.[12] The negotiated settlement approach to resolving western water conflicts was part of that revolution.

Although the negotiated settlement process has yielded some success stories—the negotiated settlement on the Carson and Truckee Rivers arguably falls into this category—the federal government began to try alternative approaches to resolve water resource conflicts to which it is a party. It has done so for several reasons. The settlement process did not work as well as anticipated in the 1980s, when President Ronald Reagan began to urge the Department of the Interior to solve western water conflicts through negotiation.

Negotiation is not suited to every situation, either. The outcomes of some of these negotiations have been subject to criticism, especially in those cases involving Native American tribes. For these and other reasons, the federal government began to look for other creative ways to solve such conflicts.

This is evident in the approach taken in the Walker River Basin, which is both creative and unique. No other western water conflict has gone this route. It is not the result of negotiations. It is not a water importation project. It is not an interbasin transfer. It is not directed at changing water use from agriculture to municipal or industrial use. It is not a large-scale public works project aimed at improving storage and conveyance infrastructure. It is a federally funded, science-driven attempt to purchase enough water from agricultural users in the Walker Basin to preserve Walker Lake, while minimizing or mitigating economic and ecological impacts to the region.

Part II

The Walker River Basin

Chapter Eight

Contemporary Issues in
the Walker River Basin

Mason and Smith Valleys are part of Lyon County, one of the fastest-growing counties in the nation. From 2000 to 2010, the population of Lyon County grew from 34,501 to 51,980.[1] Such growth and development have increased the competition for water resources in the Walker River Basin. Part of that pressure came from the Walker River Paiute Tribe, which is allied with the federal government in litigation to obtain more water rights for the reservation; fishing, recreation, and environmental interests also want to see that Walker Lake is restored and preserved.

Walker Lake is one of the six larger natural terminus lakes in western North America. It is also one of three desert terminus lakes with a freshwater fishery. The river and the lake are facing serious issues. The river is overallocated, meaning that not all the demands on the river can be met, even in normal water years. Because irrigated agriculture in the Mason and Smith Valleys consumes a significant part of the river upstream from the lake, the lake has been steadily declining. The lake level dropped from a historic (1882) high elevation of 4,083 feet above mean sea level to 3,934 feet above msl, which translates into a 149-foot drop in lake depth and a decrease in total lake volume from approximately 9.0 to 1.7 million acre-feet. Consequent changes in water quality have impaired the entire lake ecosystem. The original genetic strain of Lahontan cutthroat trout in the lake is extinct, and the lake has been stocked with a different strain of LCT. The major food source for the existing LCT is the tui chub, which the lake ecosystem is increasingly unable to support. The lake naturally experiences a buildup of total dissolved solids, particularly salts. TDS concentrations are more than 13,000 milligrams per liter, up from 1882 recordings of 2,560 mg/l. Studies show that "concentrations approaching 16,000 mg/l would result in a 100% mortality rate for the lake's Lahontan cutthroat trout."[2] If the salinity issue is not addressed in the near future, the lake will cease being a sustainable habitat for LCT and migratory waterfowl. In 2004 water quantity and quality issues caused all of the LCT in the lake to die. Since that time, the tribe has been stocking the lake with a different strain of LCT. In 2006 the US Bureau of Reclamation asserted that the lake was on the verge of environmental collapse.

All of these factors combined to focus political attention on the Walker River system. Senator Harry Reid's interest in preserving Nevada's desert terminus lakes is long-standing, as has already been demonstrated. At the time he resurrected the idea of an interstate compact in 1987, he deliberately chose to leave the Walker Basin out of that process for a variety of reasons, including the fact that the history and context of the Walker River and Lake required a different approach. Additionally, the federal government's only presence in the Walker Basin was the US Geological Survey gauging stations, advocacy on behalf of the Walker River Paiute Tribe, and an interest in maintaining trout fisheries with nonindigenous hatchery stocks. Moreover, the irrigation system in Walker Basin was privately developed, owned, and operated. Its diversion works and irrigation canal systems were constructed by individual landowners and are managed by several ditch companies and the Walker River Irrigation District. By 2007 there were approximately 110,850 acres of land in production in the basin, and WRID provided surface and storage rights for some 80,000 of those acres.[3] Increased conflict over water in the Walker Basin led to a 2003 federal district court– supervised and –sponsored mediation among stakeholders representing the Walker Lake Paiute Tribe; the Walker River Irrigation District; Lyon County, Nevada; Mineral County, Nevada; Mono County, California; the Walker River Working Group; the States of California and Nevada; and the federal government. Recognizing that more than three years of mediation efforts had produced no agreement on any of the basic issues, the Walker River Paiute Tribe withdrew from mediation in 2006, followed several months later by Mineral County and the Walker River Working Group. Consequently, the stay that had been placed on lawsuits challenging the provisions of Decree C-125 (1936), one of the two major decrees governing water allocation and use issues in the Walker Basin,[4] was lifted by the court, thereby permitting the parties to resume litigation.

As early as 1993, Senator Reid sought help from conservation biologists at the University of Nevada, Reno, in establishing baseline conditions for flora, fauna, and water quality of the Walker River Basin, on which future federal actions could be taken. That research was continued through 2004 and helped inform future policy developments regarding Walker Lake. Eventually, Reid sought —and received—authorization for a federally funded water rights acquisitions program to purchase water from "willing sellers" to deliver to the lake. That authorization came from PL 109-103, the Energy and Water Development Appropriations Act, which Congress passed on November 19, 2005.

Chapter Nine

The Road to the Walker Basin Project

The paths to passage of PL 101-618, which produced the negotiated settlement, and PL 109-103, which resulted in the Walker Basin Project, are similar in the sense that both involved subtle legislative maneuvers. In the last days of the 1989 legislative session, the negotiated settlement was in jeopardy when Congress rejected the omnibus water bill of which it was a part. Anticipating such rejection, Senator Harry Reid had also introduced the negotiated settlement as a stand-alone water bill. Sensing that the controversial bill might draw unwanted attention from oppositional colleagues, he attached the negotiated settlement to the comparatively innocuous Fallon Shoshone Paiute bill—and the bill passed largely unnoticed, even to those who had worked so diligently on it.

The Energy and Water Development Appropriation Act illustrates how funding is shifted in the federal legislative process. Although the general intent of the original legislation was kept—addressing water issues in the West—the place of expenditure of those funds was altered, as were the mechanisms that would be used to achieve the final policy goal (saving Walker Lake). The end result included the funding of the Walker Basin Project. Here, Reid sought not only to end another water war among agricultural, municipal, Native American, and environmental interests, but to do so in an ecologically and economically responsive manner. Reid achieved this through an iterative legislative process.

On May 13, 2002, Congress passed PL 107-171, the Farm Security and Rural Investment Act of 2002 (known hereafter as the Farm Bill), a five-year authorization for all of the programs under the

Department of Agriculture. Section 2507 of the Farm Bill authorized the secretary of agriculture to transfer $200 million to the Bureau of Reclamation's Water and Related Resources account, to be used by ten western states to address water quality issues. Each participating state was to receive $20 million. That law stipulated that the funds shall "remain available until expended" (Section 2507[a][2]). To gain consensus in Congress on the $200 million price tag, Section 2507 prohibited these funds from being used either to purchase or to lease water rights. This prohibition was intended to address concerns articulated by agricultural interests, notably the American Farm Bureau Federation and the Walker River Irrigation District, that government purchasing or leasing of water rights in farming communities would result in water being put to nonfarming uses.

It turned out that nine of those states were not interested in accepting this money because of the restrictions that might have come with it—and because it was perceived as an unwelcome intrusion into state and local matters. Reid then began to redirect that money to Nevada as part of his ongoing efforts to resolve the water wars in northern Nevada and preserve its desert terminus lakes.

The following year, Congress enacted PL 108-7, the Omnibus Appropriations Bill. Section 207 of this bill appropriated money from Section 2507 of the 2002 Farm Bill to provide water and assistance to the three desert terminus lakes in northern Nevada, including $1 million to create a fish hatchery at Walker Lake to benefit the Walker River Paiute Tribe. Additionally, $2 million was provided in equal shares to the states of Nevada and California, the Truckee Meadows Water Authority, and the Pyramid Lake Paiute Tribe to further implement the provisions of the negotiated settlement of 1990. Finally, Section 207(b) authorized the secretary of the interior to provide financial assistance to state and local public agencies, Native American tribes, nonprofit organizations, and individuals to carry out the terms of Section 207 of the Omnibus bill and Section 2507 of PL 107-171 (the 2002 Farm Bill). Notably, however, Section 207 of the Omnibus bill did *not* include a prohibition against using these funds to purchase or lease water rights, thereby rendering the prior prohibition moot and enabling a water rights acquisitions program in the Walker Basin—a subtle but significant change.

Additional money from the 2002 Farm Bill was made available to Nevada when Congress passed the Energy and Water Development Appropriations Act of 2004 (PL 108-137). Section 207 of that act provided $2.5 million to the state of Nevada to purchase water rights in Lahontan Valley to improve Carson Lake and Pasture, "notwithstanding" the prohibition against the same contained in Section 2507 of the 2002 Farm Bill. This act concludes by stating, as did Section 207(b) of the 2003 Omnibus Appropriation Bill, that the secretary of the interior is authorized to provide financial assistance to state and local public agencies, Native American tribes, nonprofit organizations, and individuals to carry out the provisions of both this section and Section 2507 of the Farm Bill.

In November 2005, Congress passed PL 109-103, the Energy and Water Development Appropriations Act. Section 208 directed the secretary of the interior (under the provisions of Section 2507 of the Farm Bill of 2002) to provide not more than $70 million to the University of Nevada to accomplish the following goals: "(A) to acquire from willing sellers land, water appurtenant to the land, and related interests in the Walker River Basin, Nevada; and (B) to establish and administer an agricultural and natural resources center, the mission of which shall be to undertake research, restoration, and educational activities in the Walker River Basin relating to—(i) innovative agricultural water conservation; (ii) cooperative programs for environmental restoration; (iii) fish and wildlife habitat restoration; and (iv) wild horse and burro research and adoption marketing" (Section 208 [a]). Section 208(b) of PL 109-103 specified that the secretary of the interior would provide $10 million for a water lease and purchase program for the Walker River Paiute Tribe; the water would be purchased from "willing sellers." That program had to be designed to maximize water conveyances to Walker Lake and located only within the reservation.

Section 208(c) provided $10 million for tamarisk eradication, riparian restoration, and channel restoration efforts within the Walker River Basin, "with priority given to activities that are expected to result in the greatest increased water flows to the lake." It also provided $5 million to the US Fish and Wildlife Service, the Walker River Paiute Tribe, and the Nevada Division of Wildlife to complete the design and implementation of the Western Inland Trout Initiative and Fishery Improvements in the state of Nevada, with an emphasis on the Walker River Basin.

Anticipating potential bureaucratic inertia and possible public opposition to what became the Walker Basin Project, the act stated that "for each day after June 3, 2006, on which the Bureau of Reclamation fails to comply with subsections (a), (b) and (c), the total amount made available for salaries and expenses of the Bureau of Reclamation shall be reduced by $100,000 per day" (Section 208[d]). This is a very unusual move, one that, to my knowledge, had never been used before. Clearly, Reid was determined to get this project under way as soon as possible. Reclamation initiated a planning process that led to the commitment of the appropriated funds to the University of Nevada before the deadline.

The provisions of Section 28 of PL 109-103 were implemented through a collaborative effort of the University of Nevada, Reno; the Desert Research Institute; and the Nevada System of Higher Education. UNR and DRI provided the scientific expertise for the Walker Basin Project, and NSHE coordinated the project through the Office of the Chancellor.

Broad oversight was provided by the NSHE Walker Basin Working Group, which consisted of Mike Collopy, director of the Academy for the Environment and cochair of the Walker Basin Project Study Group; Milt Glick, UNR president; Marc Johnson, UNR provost; Dan Klaich, NSHE executive vice chancellor and chair of the Executive Steering Committee; Chris Maples, DRI executive vice president for research and chief science officer; Jim Thomas, DRI associate research professor and director of DRI's Center for Watersheds and Environmental Sustainability and cochair of the Walker Basin Project Study Group; Steve Wells, DRI vice president for research; and

John V. White, professor of law at the Boyd School of Law at the University of Nevada, Las Vegas. At Reid's request, Mary Conelly, Reid's state director, and Robert Dickens, UNR director of governmental affairs, were included as ex-officio members.

UNR chose to centrally manage the project through its Academy for the Environment. The academy, established in 2004, was an interdisciplinary institution whose mission was to develop, improve, and coordinate environmental teaching, research, and service at UNR. DRI's share of the work was administered through its Center for Watersheds and Environmental Sustainability.

The appropriations legislation sought to utilize the natural resource management expertise of faculty at UNR and DRI. This expertise included hydrology, remote imaging, arid land and soils analysis, alternative crops and water quality assessment, limnology, and terminus lake fisheries.

The policy goal of this appropriation was to deliver water to Walker Lake to address the increase in lake salinity and eventually raise the water level such that the lake could sustain a robust Lahontan cutthroat trout population and migratory waterfowl, while maintaining—and perhaps even improving—the ecology and economy of the Walker Basin.

Before the research and acquisitions processes could begin, an acquisitions plan and budget were developed to serve as a long-term "road map" for the project. Eighty percent of the funds (fifty-six million dollars) was budgeted for the acquisitions program, with the other fourteen million dollars going toward research and other aspects of the project. The plan anticipated that the acquisitions process would occur over three stages: the planning and preacquisitions period (January 2007–December 2008), the option and due-diligence period (January–December 2009), and the acquisitions and stewardship phrase (beginning in 2010).[1]

UNR and DRI issued internal requests for proposals, soliciting research that would contribute to the goals of the project. Those submitted underwent a two-phase review process. The first phase was an internal peer review, judging proposals against the policy directives found in the legislation and appropriations. The second phase was an external review by the Bureau of Reclamation and Senator Reid's staff. Successful proposals were forged into collaborative research teams, with a principal investigator leading each team. At the end of that process, thirteen projects were selected for funding.

Chapter Ten

The Walker Basin Project

UNR and DRI selected thirteen projects for funding. Ten of these were scientific studies "to evaluate the present status of Walker Lake in reference to its [plant and animal life, physical properties, and geological features] and to evaluate changes in those conditions that may occur in response to changes in water delivery and management practices."[1] These studies were conducted in support of the primary policy goal outlined in the legislation: to purchase water from willing sellers in the basin and deliver that water to Walker Lake.

Nevada water law has only recently provided incentive for agricultural water conservation. Nevada's long-standing policy had been "use it or lose it." Water scarcity in an arid environment prompted farmers to confirm their rights' validity through using them as completely as possible. The unintended result was the cultivation of water-intensive crops customary to the region but lacking sensitivity to conservation. However, the Nevada Revised Statutes in 2005, 2007, and 2011 included the leasing and conservation of water as "beneficial" uses (NRS 333.550). The Walker Basin Project would not have been possible without these changes to Nevada water law.

Two studies were conducted to support the acquisitions process. The first was the development of a Geographic Information System database as a "framework for linking water rights with water distribution networks and points of diversion for the Walker Basin. . . . The resulting GIS database included data on climate, water flows, water rights, groundwater-surface water interactions, irrigation practices . . . and high resolution digital imaging, [as well as] aspects of climate and evaporation from different water sources."[2] It also included social and economic data sets from federal, state, and local agencies; remote sensing imagery; elevation data from the US Geological Survey; and soils and agricultural information from the US Department of Agriculture.[3] This database was constructed to support many project components, especially the water-flow model. All of the data in the GIS database are available to the public.

The GIS database's surface and groundwater information was used to develop a water-flow model (also known as the decision support tool) to "evaluate the effectiveness of proposed acquisitions of water rights . . . to increase water delivery to the Walker Lake."[4] Interpretation of the data yielded information about not only the deliverability of water to Walker Lake, but the relationships between junior and senior water rights, potential leasing programs, and water banking.[5] Options to purchase water from willing sellers would be exercised only if it could be verified that the acquired water was deliverable to the lake. In a river system that is overappropriated, is dominated by upstream agricultural enterprises, and whose irrigation system is privately owned and managed, knowing whether an acquired water right can be delivered to the lake is crucial.

According to Mike Collopy, cochair of the Walker Basin Study Group and director of the Academy for the Environment, the water-flow model is "one of the most exciting developments" to emerge from the project. It is essentially a software program that describes how the "snowpack in the Sierra ultimately melts and finds its way through the Walker River and into the lake, accounting for all the agricultural uses along the way . . . which enables us to better understand the consequences of different kinds of water rights purchases."[6]

Doug Boyle, associate professor at DRI and principal investigator for this part of the project, noted that such models are used all over the world for a variety of purposes. This model is unique, however, in that it brings together a number of "different, very complicated models that all work together to help us understand the hydrology of the Walker River system. They are set up to run different scenarios based on potential future water rights acquisitions. . . . The water-flow model can serve many different purposes. The hope is that this tool will be used in the future by water managers in the Walker Basin to improve their operations and get the most bang for their bucks."[7]

Scott Tyler, professor, Department of Geological Sciences and Engineering at UNR, used "distributive sensing" fiber-optic cable to measure stream temperatures throughout the system in order to better understand groundwater inflows and outflows to the Walker River. According to Collopy, "These measurements permitted assessment of where gains to channel flow were occurring [so that] inflow zones to the river can be identified based on temperature differences, permitting efficient sampling for determining potential salinity loading to the river."[8]

Tyler's group discovered that the same fiber-optic cable can be used to measure soil temperatures. They buried cable lines about six inches deep on some of the acreage that another team was using to grow alternative crops, which enabled them to read the soil temperature across a whole field. This information could be used, in turn, to identify which parts of a given field need to watered and when. Farmers using this technology can "optimize production by just knowing when and where to irrigate different parts of the field."[9]

Four research projects addressed potential consequences to agriculture, ecosystems, and the economy in the basin as water is acquired for the lake. One of these established a benchmark for the environmental and ecological health of the lake and the river. Scientists gathered baseline data about the river, the lake, and lands that are riparian to both. Sudeep Chandra, associate professor of limnology and fisheries conservation at UNR, concluded that the river is "on the fence," halfway between healthy and unhealthy.[10] The hope is that "enough" water will be purchased or leased (or both) not only to maintain the ecology of the lake but to improve it.

Chandra's team also discovered that "the biological resources that the fishes utilize . . . indicate that the fishes obtain a large part of their energy from bottom near-shore invertebrates" during winter.[11]

The other biological resources come from the lake's surface area in the summer. In order to make better management decisions, Chandra's team recommended that the lake be monitored year-round, on both the surface area and at the bottom, in order to understand their life cycles and growth.[12]

Don Sada, aquatic ecologist at DRI, concluded that the river and its riparian system are in good condition; this is good news, since the lake and the river are part of one system. Sada also indicated that it "might not take much change in the management of the system to improve conditions on the lake."[13]

The second project addressing potential consequences to the basin identified the "economic potential" for alternative crops that used less water than is required to grow alfalfa. Approximately 92 percent of the acreage in the basin is used to grow alfalfa or grass hay. The alternative-crops team grew eight crops and calculated the costs and returns on each, using water and soil data. Crops tested included vegetable crops, a variety of grains and grasses, and wine grapes. The team wanted to discover whether these crops would be profitable over a one-hundred-year time span. Kyndra Curtis, assistant professor in the Department of Resource Economics at UNR, reported that "all of the crops they planted, except for switchgrass, could be just as profitable as alfalfa and maybe more so."[14] Those crops tested could be grown using one to three a-f-y of water, compared to the four a-f-y required to grow alfalfa.

The most promising alternative crop was teff, which is a grass. Its seeds are used to make a type of Ethiopian bread (*injera*), which is in very high demand there. Jay Davison, Cooperative Extension scientist at UNR whose specialty is production agriculture, said it "takes eighty-five to ninety days to grow. [Cooperative Extension] first brought teff to Nevada about seven years ago, and we have been growing it ever since. It is a plant that is well suited to Nevada and uses one-half to two-thirds of the water that alfalfa does."[15] It is one of the few crops that Cooperative Extension brought to the state that has been widely adopted. According to Davison, "Farmers in four counties are growing it, either as a grain (500–600 acres) or for forage (700–800 acres)."[16] Davison expects this acreage to yield about eight hundred thousand pounds of teff seed, each acre of which can gross one thousand dollars for the farmer.

The alternative-crops team took information from a larger economic model and "put it in a user-friendly electronic spreadsheet that producers can use. This tool can be used by farmers to determine the optimum mix of crops that they could grow profitably. Farmers could also determine how much water and fertilizer would be required for different growing scenarios."[17]

The team also experimented with using native plants and shrubs to revegetate land that does not have enough water on it to grow crops profitably. When water is sold and removed from land and such land is not revegetated, invasive species, soil erosion, and dust become major problems. This research also studied methods for revegetating acreage as farmers adopt crops that use less water or sell water rights to the project.

A third research project in this grouping assessed probable plant, soil, and water interactions that occur as a function of changes in water use. Another sought to provide farmers in the basin with an estimate of how much water they might be able to offer to the market for lease or sale.

Because of the university's land-grant status[18] and long-standing commitments in the Walker River Basin, some study components involved evaluations of the local economy and provided an economic development plan by collaborating with public and private interests in the Mason and Smith Valleys. The goal is to provide locally controlled tools to guide local business development. One water-conserving business idea that was evaluated was a landscape nursery for Great Basin–hardened plant species serving northern Nevada horticultural markets. Another focused on hydroponic greenhouse cash crops. Development and attraction of small businesses in sectors missing in the local economy were other goals.

Three projects pertained to project coordination, communications, and outreach. The Nevada System of Higher Education Working Group oversaw these projects. Western Development and

Storage, a Los Angeles firm experienced in water storage, conservation, transfers, and banking, was selected to coordinate the water
rights acquisitions process during the early stages of the project.
These thirteen projects were funded at $10,167,000.

"Saving" Walker Lake required that the government and the
potentially affected parties work together: the Walker River Paiute
Tribe, agricultural interests (WRID), environmental groups, relevant
federal and state agencies, and the general public. Thus, the Walker
Basin Project needed to keep the affected parties informed and
engaged from the very beginning.

Engaging the Public

A Stakeholders Group was formed in late 2006 to represent major
interests in the basin. This group included two at-large members
selected by Reid and Senator John Ensign and representatives of
the Nevada Department of Conservation and Natural Resources,
the US Fish and Wildlife Service, Lyon County, the Bureau of Land
Management, the Nevada Division of State Lands, the Walker River
Paiute Tribe, the hunting and fishing community, Mono County,
the California Department of Water Resources, the Walker River
Irrigation District, the Walker Lake Working Group, and Mineral
County. Quarterly meetings were scheduled for the Stakeholders
Group, the cochairs of the Walker Basin Study Group, communication teams from UNR and DRI, the project coordinator, and the chair
of the Working Group. The public and the press were encouraged to
attend these meetings and to ask questions and provide input.

In addition to the stakeholders' meetings, the communications
team created a website that included a brief history of Walker Lake
and its current status; the legislation that authorized the $70 million
expenditure; project goals; the list of stakeholders, along with con-
tact information; and descriptions of the research projects, including monthly updates. The idea was to create transparent, ongoing,
two-way communications.

Initial opposition to the project in Lyon County was fierce. The
first stakeholders' meeting attracted a standing-room-only crowd.

An overview of the Walker Basin Project was presented, followed by a question-and-answer period. Instead of inviting people to speak, the meeting facilitator asked that they submit questions on index cards. The attendees seemed puzzled by this, but some nonetheless filled out cards and passed them to the facilitator, who began to read the cards aloud, so that members of the project team could answer the questions posed.

The attendees apparently interpreted this as a tactic to keep them from voicing their concerns, many of which could not be stated on a three-by-five-inch index card. They wanted to speak not only to the project team, but to one another. The crowd began to murmur, a murmuring that turned into shouts questioning the necessity of the project, dismissing the Walker Lake Paiute Tribe, and challenging the integrity of the scientists involved in the project. One farmer angrily announced the "three biggest lies ever told," one of which was "the government is here to help you." Another charged that UNR was using black helicopters to spy on farmers in Walker Basin. (It turns out that there were indeed black helicopters flying over the area; the pilots were in training for eventual deployment to Afghanistan.)

Claims were made that the Stakeholders Group did not represent the "real" stakeholders in the valley, that community input was not being taken seriously, and that the research would yield a predetermined set of recommendations. A lawyer representing agricultural and domestic well interests in Mason Valley observed that "the last thing that Nevada needs is to turn the prosperous Mason and Smith Valleys into a mirror image of the now relatively deserted Owens Valley."[19]

Jim Sanford, former Mason Valley editor and publisher, wrote many opinion pieces for the *Mason Valley News*. The headlines from these pieces illustrate the sentiment in the basin in 2007: "Guest Shot . . . Any Fight Left in Mason and Smith Valleys?" (July 13, 2007); "A Wake Up Call . . . If You Don't Think Games Are Being Played, You're Naïve" (July 20, 2007); "Saving Walker Lake Really a 'Feel Good' Proposal? Picture Mason Valley Without 80% of Its

Farms" (October 5, 2007); "Two Cents Worth: Fair Market Value of Walker River Water Is $2,500 Per Acre Foot?" (November 16, 2007); and "Two Cents Worth: Is Harry Reid Contributing to Global Warming?" (December 21, 2007).

Such criticism began to wane as research team members started their fieldwork, which resulted in positive interactions between the locals and the researchers. One Lyon County farmer, who had consistently opposed any federal role in local agriculture, eventually leased his property to the project to conduct research on water-conserving crops.

Research designs and preliminary results were presented at community forums and stakeholder meetings. For example, an economic analysis of marketable crops was completed and presented to stakeholders, including farmers, some of whom sought new crops and additional markets. Questions and comments from those in attendance were solicited. Those who wanted to speak were given the floor. Individuals from Lyon County also began to communicate with the project coordinators and scientists through e-mails and telephone calls.

As communication increased, newspaper editorials became more supportive of letting the research teams conduct the science and see where it led. Even Jim Sanford began taking a more moderate stance:

Welcome to 2008. Enough saber rattling. Time to work toward a more palatable solution concerning the Walker River Basin Project. . . . The basic issue is that there is a lawsuit in the courts seeking changes in the amount of water the downstream tribe receives, plus what can be labeled "an environmental issue" at the end of the system [Walker Lake]. . . . Both these issues have to be addressed because of the lawsuit and proposed federal legislation. . . . It's 2008, we have to do something more [than keep calling UNR and DRI names]; time's a wasting.[20]

Sanford later observed that the community had come to realize that change was coming whether they liked it or not—and they might as well become part of and help shape that change. Sanford also indicated that this change of heart was in part the result of the community's coming to trust the researchers and the objectivity of their research. They also became more accepting of the idea that the research might show how to sustain agriculture and diversify the economy while delivering water to Walker Lake.

Water Acquisitions

The "willing sellers" language in the legislation was intended to dispel any concerns about land or water rights being taken forcibly. Although such language did not prevent vocal opposition, it did generate inquiries from landowners interested in selling water rights. Some outspoken opponents to the Walker Basin Project eventually collaborated with researchers on alternative crop and natural revegetation projects and even made their land available for demonstration projects.

Water acquisition from willing sellers was pursued in parallel with the research project. Willing sellers entered into private negotiations with water resource experts and water rights attorneys. By late 2009, eleven option agreements were being formulated, and Phase One of the Walker Basin Project research was essentially complete.[21] In October 2009, Congress established the Walker Basin Restoration Program, to assume responsibility for continued research, conservation, and ecological restoration in the Walker Basin in order to restore and maintain Walker Lake. In that latter capacity, the restoration program was tasked with pursuing water acquisitions that could be delivered to the lake. The National Fish and Wildlife Foundation was designated the lead agency for developing and implementing that program.

The Walker Basin Restoration Program

NFWF is a 501(c)(3) nonprofit organization that was created by Congress in 1984 to "direct . . . public conservation dollars to the most pressing environmental needs and match . . . those investments with private funds."[22] The Walker Basin Restoration Program is designed to restore ecological health to Walker Lake, in cooperation with the Bureau of Reclamation. It is funded by the Desert Terminus Lakes program.

In accepting responsibility for the Walker Basin Restoration Program, NFWF agreed to accept full "responsibility for all dimensions of the acquisitions program portion of the Nevada System of Higher Education's Walker Basin Project."[23] In that capacity, NFWF negotiated purchase and sale agreements on six permanent[24] water acquisition deals, at a total purchase price of $23.5 million. To date, NFWF has acquired more than 31 cubic feet per second of natural-flow decree rights, 2,500 a-f of storage water rights, 3,715 a-f of groundwater rights, and nearly 1,900 acres of land. NFWF continues to explore new agreements with dozens of potential sellers who had contacted it since early 2010. By that time, more people had come to see that the situation need not be a "zero-sum game pitting the lake against the irrigators."[25]

In April 2010, NFWF and WRID reached an agreement on a demonstration water leasing program "to take advantage of anticipated high river flows. . . . [T]he agreement provide[s] funds for landowners to be paid to leave such 'flood waters' in the river throughout the spring snowmelt season."[26] That water would have otherwise been diverted to fields and farms prematurely in the growing season. Approximately two-thirds of WRID's 80,000 eligible acres are enrolled in the program.[27] In high-water years, a substantial amount of water would be delivered to Walker Lake.

Besides acquiring water rights, NFWF has undertaken several other related tasks authorized under the Walker Basin Restoration Program. One of its other priorities includes soil conservation and revegetation on lands where water has been removed. For example, a large-scale revegetation effort has been undertaken on 177 acres in Smith Valley, which is now being implemented by the Smith Valley Conservation District with money provided by NFWF. It also provided funding to the Mason Valley Conservation District to help with the various stewardship efforts in Mason Valley. These efforts build upon earlier research conducted by UNR and DRI. Scientists from both institutions continue to work on revegetation in the basin.

NFWF also provided grants to UNR and DRI scientists to conduct Phase Two research in the basin,[28] including continued modeling of surface-groundwater interactions to support future water leasing and acquisitions, research on alternative crops, continued economic evaluations of alternative crops, and overall ecological monitoring of the Walker River. Conservation funds were also provided to the Nevada Department of Wildlife's Mason Valley Management area "as part of an ongoing project to conserve water at the north end of the Management Area for eventual discharge into the Walker River."[29] Funds were provided for the City of Yerington to remove sediment from the Yerington Weir to improve conveyance of leased and acquired water and to the Walker River Paiute Tribe to improve conveyance of water through the Walker River Paiute Reservation, so that leased and acquired water could be more easily delivered to Walker Lake.

Concluding Observations

The Walker Basin Project represents a sophisticated attempt to develop and test scientific tools with which to assist achievement of the public policy goals stated in the legislation and as further identified in the Walker Basin Project. Data have been gathered, databases have been built, water-flow models have been tested, demonstration of alternative crops is ongoing, use of natural vegetation to control dust and invasive weeds is being pursued, and economic impact analyses have been conducted that yielded recommendations for future economic development. NFWF continues to work with local citizens to produce a set of accommodations that conserve natural resources, local communities, and a rural Nevada lifestyle. NFWF will continue to implement the Walker River Restoration Program through the foreseeable future.

~~~~~~

Chapter Eleven

Into the Future

The United States is a nation of two mind-sets, constantly juxtapos-
ing the individual against the group. This is especially true in the
West, where a frontier mentality and "rugged individualism" have
deep historical roots. Westerners tend to focus on the rights of the
individual, often at the expense of the common good. This orientation is perhaps most greatly reflected in efforts to determine how
best to allocate and use our water. Such a struggle has resulted in
decades of litigation among competing interests: agricultural,
urban, Native American, and environmental. In the two cases presented in this book, litigation was pursued for more than one hundred years. The problem with a litigious approach is that it takes
untold millions of dollars, it creates "enemies," and the outcome
is always uncertain. It makes long-term planning impossible. Both
cases covered in this book clearly illustrate the points made above.

In the 1980s, the federal government began to encourage those
involved in water resource conflicts in the West to embrace negotiation as an alternative approach to litigation. Senator Harry Reid led
the charge in the negotiations that led to PL 101-618. The negotiated
settlement and the Truckee River Operating Agreement produced
win-win outcomes. The provisions of that law are not "fully" implemented, but progress is being made. The Truckee-Carson Irrigation District and the Pyramid Lake Paiute Tribe are in discussions.
The expectation is that they will resolve their differences in the near
future. When that happens, TCID will drop the lawsuits that it initiated against the federal government after the settlement became
law.

The federal government will soon initiate a lawsuit requesting that the court alter the Truckee River General Electric Decree so that relevant provisions of PL 101-618 can be incorporated into it. It has already done that for the Orr Ditch Decree, and changes to that decree have been made. The Cities of Reno and Sparks and Washoe County do not have the money to purchase the additional 3,200 a-f of water that they "owe" the Truckee River. Given how much time, money, and effort the federal government has invested in this settlement, it is not unreasonable to assume that it will provide the funding to purchase that amount of water on behalf of these three entities. When all of these issues are settled, the law will be deemed "fully" implemented, and the Pyramid Lake Paiute Tribe will be able to access the money in its economic development trust fund, along with the interest that fund has generated, which is more than one hundred million dollars as of this writing.

The negotiated settlement has been hailed by many not only as a success story but as a model for others to emulate. Given that there are twenty-two such negotiations under way, this might be an alluring prospect in some of those cases. That model is not suited for all major water conflicts in the West, however.

The Walker River system required an approach suited to a privately owned and operated irrigation system. Reid secured passage of "desert terminus legislation" that resulted in a seventy-million-dollar grant to the University of Nevada to undertake the "Walker Basin Project," which was a sophisticated, science-driven program to purchase water from willing sellers to deliver to Walker Lake. Phase One of that project was completed in 2009, and responsibility for continued water acquisitions, among other things, was transferred to the Walker Basin Restoration Program. The National Fish and Wildlife Foundation is the lead agency for carrying out that program. Six options to purchase water have been exercised. Dozens more are in the works. Although it is difficult to determine how much water will be "enough" to "save" Walker Lake, estimates range from 50,000 to 85,000 a-f-y.

Was the Walker Basin Project a success? I believe so, at least in the short term. The communities in Mason and Smith Valleys were involved from the beginning, a significant aspect of "civic science"—science conducted that affects a specific community. An ecological baseline was developed for the river and the lake that can be used to make better management decisions. Out of the eight alternative crops tested, seven prove to be suitable to the basin. Each of these, if adopted, would yield profits at least as high as those obtained by growing alfalfa—and would require significantly less water. A new use for fiber-optic cable was discovered; when buried under a field, a sensor informs a farmer which parts of his field need to be watered and when, enabling the farmer to optimize production. An economic development plan was created for the basin. And a water acquisitions program is in place. The long-term success of *that* program remains to be seen. Might these two approaches be appropriate for resolving other water "wars" in the future? Yes. But we must continue to discover other innovative ways to resolve western water conflicts. The clear message that comes from this book is that a "one size fits all" approach does not work. We need to tailor the approach to any given water conflict to the specific nature of that conflict.

Notes

~~~~~~~~~~~~~~~~~~~~~~~~~~

Chapter One | Water, People, and Politics

1. US Senate, *Providing for the Settlement of Water Rights Claims of the Fallon Paiute Shoshone Indian Tribes,* 9.

2. Article XXII, 1987, 3.

3. Troy R. Johnson, "Roots of Contemporary Native American Activism."

4. Joane Nagel, *American Indian Ethnic Renewal: Red Power and the Resurgence of Identity and Culture;* Ward Churchill, *Struggle for the Land: Native North American Resistance to Genocide, Ecocide, and Colonization.*

Chapter Two | Reclamation Policy—Trials and Tribulations

1. Donald J. Pisani, *Water, Land and the Law in the West: The Limits of Public Policy, 1850–1920,* 182.

2. William D. Rowley, *Bureau of Reclamation: Origins and Growth to 1945,* 83.

3. Ibid., 81.

4. Gary A. Horton, *Truckee River Chronology: A Chronological History of Lake Tahoe and the Truckee River and Related Water Issues,* III-1 (emphasis added).

5. Daniel C. McCool, *Command of the Waters: Iron Triangles, Federal Water Development, and Indian Water.*

6. Gary A. Horton, *Carson River Chronology: A Chronological History of the Carson River and Related Water Issues,* I-7.

7. Ibid.

8. Final Decree, *U.S. v. Orr Water Ditch Co.,* in Equity Docket A-3 (D. Nev. 1944).

9. Horton, *Truckee River Chronology,* 16–17.

10. *Winters v. United States,* 207 U.S. 564, 28 S. Ct. 207, 52 L. Ed. 340.

11. *Nevada v. United States,* 463 U.S. 110 (1983).

12. William Joe Simonds, *The Newlands Project,* 13.

13. Ibid.

14. Ibid., 13–14.

15. Horton, *Truckee River Chronology*, I-7.

16. US Census, 1900–1990.

17. US Senate, *Providing for the Settlement*, 13.

18. 84th Cong., 2nd sess., 1956, H. Rep. 2055, 4–5.

19. Horton, *Carson River Chronology*, I-68.

20. According to Horton, *Truckee River Chronology*, I-42, 43, *benchland* is a term for "sandy-gravelly well-drained soils overlying a deep water table that exhibits relatively low water-holding capacity and rapid infiltration of irrigation water." *Bottomland* refers to "rich, loamy or fine-textured and poorly drained soils, overlying a shallow water table or adjacent to a stream or lake that has relatively good water-holding capacity and which is slow to moderate infiltration of irrigation water."

21. Ibid.

Chapter Three | The California-Nevada Interstate Compact

1. W. Turrentine Jackson and Donald J. Pisani, *A Case Study in Interstate Resource Management: The California-Nevada Water Controversy, 1955–1968*, 255.

2. John M. Townley, *Turn This Water into Gold: The Story of the Newlands Project*, 80.

3. Patricia Zell, oral history interview by Donald B. Seney.

4. Joseph Ely, oral history interview by Donald B. Seney.

5. Ibid.

6. Ibid.

7. Donald B. Seney, "The Changing Political Fortunes of the Truckee-Carson Irrigation District."

8. Robert Pelcyger, oral history interview by Donald B. Seney.

9. Zell, interview by Seney.

10. Public Law 89-699 (1966).

11. *Nevada v. United States*, 463 U.S. (1983) at 145.

12. US Senate, *Providing for the Settlement*, 16.

13. Fed. Reg. 3098; 43 C.F.R. 418.

14. Pelcyger, oral history interview by Seney.

15. *Pyramid Lake Paiute Tribe of Indians v. Rogers C. B. Morton, et al.*, 354 F. Supp. 252 D.D.C. (1973).

16. *Truckee-Carson Irrigation District v. Secretary of the Interior,* 742 F.2d 527 (9th Cir., 1984).

17. Cert. den. 53 U.S.L.W. 3867 (June 11, 1985).

18. Horton, *Truckee River Chronology,* III-28.

19. http://www.tcid.ord, 2008.

20. Simonds, *The Newlands Project,* 19.

21. Ibid.

22. *Pyramid Lake Paiute Tribe v. Hodel,* 882 F.2d 364 (9th Cir., 1989).

23. *Carson-Truckee Water Conservancy District v. Clark,* 741 F.2d 257 (9th Cir., 1984).

24. Cert, den, 53 U.S.L.W. 386 (March 26, 1985).

25. US Senate, *Providing for the Settlement,* 2.

Chapter Four | Coming to Terms

1. Joe Gremban, oral history interview by Donald B. Seney.

2. Chester Buchanan, personal communication with the author.

3. Ibid. This figure is an estimate by the US Fish and Wildlife Service.

4. Pelcyger, oral history interview by Seney.

5. Seney, "Changing Political Fortunes."

6. Marcus Faust, oral history interview by Donald B. Seney.

7. Pelcyger, oral history interview by Seney.

8. Faust, oral history interview by Seney.

9. Zell, oral history interview by Seney.

10. Frank Dimick, interview by Glen Krutz.

11. Gremban, oral history interview by Seney.

12. Zell, oral history interview by Seney.

Chapter Five | Navigating Congressional Waters

1. US Senate, *Hearing Before the Subcommittee on Water and Power of the Committee on Energy and Natural Resources,* 115–24.

2. Faust, oral history interview by Seney.

3. Reclamation's mission statement was changed in the early 1990s to include management of water resources in an ecologically and economically sound manner and to enhance conditions for fish, wildlife, land, and cultural resources. It also assists the secretary of the interior in fulfilling its Indian trust responsibilities (http://www.usbr.gov).

4. US Senate, *Hearing Before the Subcommittee on Water and Power,* 124.

5. Thomas Jensen, oral history interview by Donald B. Seney.

6. Pelcyger, oral history interview by Seney.

7. Jensen, oral history interview by Seney.

8. Faust, oral history interview by Seney.

9. Jensen, oral history interview by Seney.

10. Zell, oral history interview by Seney.

11. Ibid.

12. Ibid.

13. Ibid.

14. Jensen, oral history interview by Seney.

15. Zell, oral history interview by Seney.

16. Jensen, oral history interview by Seney.

Chapter Six | An End in Sight?

1. Sec. 103 limits the acquisition of land and water to no more than 2,415.1 acres and 88,453.55 a-f-y, respectively.

2. http://www.plpy.nsn.us.

3. Jeff DeLong, "Giant Cutthroats Show Efforts to Restore Native Fish to Pyramid Lake Working," *Reno Gazette-Journal,* February 25, 2013.

4. Snapshot, "Return of Cutthroat Trout a Victory for Conservation," *Reno Gazette-Journal,* March 14, 2013, 1.

5. Ibid.

6. On June 11, 2001, Sierra Pacific Power Company transferred Westpac, its water purveyor at the time, to the Truckee Meadows Water Authority.

7. The federal reservoirs are Boca, Lake Tahoe, Martis Creek, Prosser Creek, and Stampede.

8. These are Donner and Independence.

9. US Department of the Interior, *Executive Summary: Truckee River Operating Agreement, Final Environmental Impact Statement.*

10. Federal Register, vol. 73, no. 235, December 5, 2008, Rules and Regulations 74031.

11. *United States of America v. the Orr Water Ditch Co., et al.,* November 11, 2008, Case No. 3:73-cv-00003-LDG.

12. Contract no. 7-07-20 0348, November 26, 1996.

13. Because the ditches and diversion canals in the Newlands Project are not lined or covered, only 45 percent of the water released from the reservoirs ever makes it to the fields; 55 percent is lost to seepage and evaporation. To attain a 75 percent efficiency rate—the percentage of released water

that actually makes it to the field—will require significant improvements on the district's delivery system.

14. *United States of America v. Board of Directors, Truckee Carson Irrigation District,* 2011 U.S. Dist. LEXIS 116239, October 6, 2011.

Chapter Seven | Staying the Course

1. Wayne Mehl, oral history interview by Donald B. Seney.

2. Leif Reid, "Ripple from the Truckee: The Case for Congressional Apportionment of Disputed Interstate Water Rights."

3. Zell, oral history interview by Seney.

4. Ely, oral history interview by Seney.

5. Sue Oldham was an attorney working with Sierra Pacific Power Company throughout this process.

6. http://www.tcid.org.

7. Pelcyger, oral history interview by Seney.

8. Lynn McConnell, oral history interview by Seney.

9. Selby Cecil passed away and was dropped from the indictment.

10. Scott Sonner, "Deal Struck in Case Against Nevada Irrigation District," *Reno Gazette-Journal,* October 16, 2009.

11. Daniel C. McCool, *Native Waters: Contemporary Indian Water Settlements and the Second Treaty Era,* 9.

12. Todd Olinger, *Trends and Directions in Federal Water Policy: A Summary of the Proceedings: Report to the Western Water Policy Review Commission,* 1.

Chapter Eight | Contemporary Issues in the Walker River Basin

1. US Census, 2010.

2. Gary A. Horton, *Walker River Chronology: A Chronological History of the Walker River and Related Water Issues,* I-12.

3. Saxon E. Sharpe, Mary E. Cablk, and James M. Thomas, *The Walker Basin, Nevada and California: Physical Environment, Hydrology, and Biology,* 6.

4. The other is Decree 731, issued in 1919; it determined the amount of water to which each entity on the West Walker was entitled, the source of the water, the area to which it is to be applied, and the propriety date for each use. It also determined water rights for the Walker River Paiute tribe. Decree C-125 recognized the provisions of Decree 731. The tribe was granted the right to divert 26.26 cfs for 180 days to irrigate 2,100 acres of land; these rights were given a priority date of 1859, the year the reservation

was created. The tribe and the federal government have banded together to obtain additional water rights for the tribe.

Chapter Nine | *The Road to the Walker Basin Project*

1. Nevada System of Higher Education, *Final Report, Phase One.*

Chapter Ten | *The Walker Basin Project*

1. Walker Basin Project, *Final Report and Documentation,* Executive Summary, 2010, iii, http://www.nevada.edu/walker.

2. Ibid., viii–ix.

3. Ibid.

4. Ibid.

5. *Water banking* is "broadly defined as an institutional mechanism that facilitates the legal transfer and market exchange of various types of surface, groundwater, and storage entitlements. In effect, the bank acts as an intermediary—or broker—bringing together buyers and sellers." West Water Research, *Publication No. 04-11-011.*

6. Mike Collopy, cochair of the Walker Basin Study Group and director of the Academy for the Environment at UNR, interview on *Preserving a Desert Treasure: Walker Basin Project* (DVD).

7. Doug Boyle, associate research professor and director of DRI's Nevada Water Research Institute, interview on ibid.

8. Collopy, interview on ibid.

9. Scott Tyler, professor, Department of Geological Sciences and Engineering, UNR, interview on ibid.

10. Sudeep Chandra, associate professor of limnology and fisheries conservation at UNR, interview on ibid.

11. Chandra, personal communication, May 19, 2013.

12. Chandra, interview on *Preserving a Desert Treasure.*

13. Don Sada, aquatic ecologist at DRI, interview on ibid.

14. Kyndra Curtis, assistant professor in the Department of Resource Economics at UNR, UNR Cooperative Extension, interview on ibid.

15. Jay Davison, area forage and alternative crops specialist, UNR Cooperative Extension, interview on ibid.

16. Ibid.

17. Curtis, interview on ibid.

18. UNR is one of fifty land-grant universities, authorized under the 1862

Morrill Land Grant Act. That act and the Nevada Constitution require UNR to maintain agricultural and outreach programs.

19. The city of Los Angeles began importing water from Owens Lake in Owens Valley, California, in 1913 (two hundred miles from LA). By 1926 the lake was completely dry, creating huge dust problems for the area.

20. Jim Sanford, "Two Cents Worth: Walker River Basin Resolution, 'Take Two,'" *Mason Valley News,* January 18, 2008, 1–2.

21. Walker Basin Research Projects, *Phase One, 2007–2009.*

22. Walker Basin Restoration Program, *Progress Report, 2010–2011.*

23. Ibid. NSHE scientists continued fine-tuning research that had been done in the Walker Basin, but NSHE ceased its efforts to acquire land and water rights.

24. NSHE had been working on eleven option agreements. When the Walker Basin Restoration Program was created in late 2009, NFWF was able to renegotiate six of these; the other five either expired or were withdrawn by the sellers.

25. *High Country News,* August 8, 2011.

26. Walker Basin Restoration Program, *Progress Report, 2010–2011.*

27. Ibid.

28. Walker Basin Project, *Current Research, 2011-2013.*

29. Walker Basin Restoration Program, *Progress Report, 2010–2011.*

Bibliography

Bates, Sarah F., et al. *Searching Out Headwaters: Change and Rediscovery in Western Water Policy*. Washington, DC: Island Press, 1993.

Bell, Craig D., and Norman K. Johnson. "State Water Laws and Federal Water Uses: The History of Conflict, the Prospects for Accommodation." *Environmental Law* 21 (1991): 1–88.

Berman, Larry, and Bruce Allen Murphy. *Approaching Democracy*. Upper Saddle River, NJ: Prentice Hall, 2003.

Bettenburg, Bill, Deputy Assistant Secretary for Indian Affairs, Department of Interior. Interview by Glen Krutz. Washington, DC, May 23, 1991.

Blackhawk, Ned. *Violence over the Land: Indians and Empires in the Early American West*. Cambridge, MA: Harvard University Press, 2006.

Boyle, Doug. Interview on *Preserving a Desert Treasure: Walker Basin Project* (DVD). Reno: University of Nevada, Reno, and the Desert Research Institute, 2009.

Brinkley, Alan. *The Unfinished Nation*. New York: McGraw-Hill, 2000.

Buchanan, Chester. Interview by Leah J. Wilds. Carson City, NV, July 6, 2008.

Bureau of Reclamation. *Summary Statistics*. Denver: Bureau of Reclamation, 1987.

Bureau of Reclamation, Mid-Pacific Region. *Managing Water in the West*. 2007. http://www.usbr.gov/mp/1bao/ocap/html.

Burness, H. S., et al. "United States Reclamation Policy and Indian Water Rights." *Natural Resources Journal* 20 (1980): 807–25.

California Department of Water Resources. *Carson River Atlas*. Sacramento: California Department of Water Resources, 1991.

———. *Truckee River Atlas*. Sacramento: Department of Water Resources, 1991.

Campana, Michael E. "Wet Water vs. Paper Water." *Water Wired,* May 27, 2009. http://www.aquadoc.typepad.com/waterwired/2009/05/wet-water-vs-paper-water.html.

Campbell, Michael, Project Manager, Sacramento District, United States Corps of Engineers. Oral history interview by Richard Acton. November 16, 2001.

Chandra, Sudeep. Interview on *Preserving a Desert Treasure: Walker Basin Project* (DVD). Reno: University of Nevada, Reno, and Desert Research Institute, 2009.

Churchill, Ward. *Struggle for the Land: Native North American Resistance to Genocide, Ecocide, and Colonization.* San Francisco: City Lights, 2002.

Clark, Jeanne Nienaber, and Daniel C. McCool. *Staking Out the Terrain: Resource Differentials Among Natural Resource Management Agencies.* Albany: State University Press of New York, 1985.

Colby, Bonnie G., Mark McGinnis, and Kent Rait. "Mitigating Environmental Externalities Through Voluntary and Involuntary Water Reallocation: Nevada's Truckee–Carson River Basin." *Natural Resource Journal* (1991): 757–83.

Colby, Bonnie G., John E. Thorson, and Sarah Britton. *Negotiating Tribal Water Rights: Fulfilling Promises in the Arid West.* Tucson: University of Arizona Press, 2006.

Collopy, Mike. Interview on *Preserving a Desert Treasure: Walker Basin Project* (DVD). Reno: University of Nevada, Reno, and the Desert Research Institute, 2009.

Conelly, Mary. Interview by Leah J. Wilds. Reno, NV, October 8, 2009.

"The Dam Builders." *Snake River Currents,* June 12, 2001, 2–3.

Davison, Jay. Interview on *Preserving a Desert Treasure: Walker Basin Project* (DVD). Reno: University of Nevada, Reno, and the Desert Research Institute, 2009.

d'Estrée, Tamara Pearson, and Bonnie Colby. *Braving the Currents: Evaluating Environmental Conflict Resolution in the River Basins of the American West.* Boston: Kluwer Academic, 2004.

Dimick, Frank, Western Relations Liaison, Bureau of Reclamation. Oral history interview by Glen Krutz. Washington, DC, May 21, 1991.

Dunlap, Riley E., and Angela G. Mertig, eds. *American Environmentalism: The U.S. Environmental Movement, 1970–1990.* Philadelphia: Taylor and Francis, 1992.

Dunn, Sandra. "Cooperative Federalism in the Acquisition of Water Rights: A Federal Practitioner's Point of View." *Pacific Law Journal* 19 (1988): 1323–38.

Elliott, Russell R. *History of Nevada.* Reno: University of Nevada Press, 1973.

Ely, Joseph, Chairman, Pyramid Lake Paiute Tribe. Oral history interview by Donald B. Seney. Mesa, AZ, May 20, 1996.

Faust, Marcus, Lobbyist, Sierra Pacific Power Company. Oral history interview by Donald B. Seney. Washington, DC, November 9, 1995.

"50, 100, & 150 Years Ago." *Scientific American* 293, no. 6 (2005): 16.

Fisher, Roger, and William Ury. *Getting to Yes: Negotiating Agreement Without Giving In.* Boston: Houghton Mifflin, 1981.

Folk-Williams, John A. "The Use of Negotiated Agreements to Resolve Water Disputes Involving Indian Water Rights." *Natural Resources Journal* 28 (Winter 1988): 63–103.

Gammon, Clive. "Lost and Found: A Fish Story." *Sports Illustrated,* November 6, 1989, 5–16.

Getches, David H. *Tribal Water Issues and the Changing Policy Landscape.* Western Water Policy Review Advisory Commission. Springfield, IL: National Technical Information Service, 1997.

Gremban, Joe, President, Sierra Pacific Power Company. Oral history interview by Donald B. Seney. Reno, NV, October 21, 1994.

Haller, Timothy G. "The Legislative Battle over the California-Nevada Interstate Compact: A Question of Might Versus Native American Right." *Nevada Historical Society Quarterly* 32, no. 3 (1989): 198–221.

Hay, Tim, Legislative Counsel, Office of Senator Reid. Oral history interview by Glen Krutz. Washington, DC, May 20, 1991.

Hebert, Tom, Water Resources Assistant, Senate Agriculture Committee. Oral history interview by Glen Krutz. Washington, DC, May 23, 1991.

Hibbard, Benjamin Horace. *A History of Public Lands Policies.* New York: Peter Smith, 1939.

Horton, Gary A. *Carson River Chronology: A Chronological History of the Carson River and Related Water Issues.* Carson City, NV: Department of Conservation and Natural Resources, 1996.

———. *Truckee River Chronology: A Chronological History of Lake Tahoe and the Truckee River and Related Water Issues.* Carson City, NV: Department of Conservation and Natural Resources, 1996.

———. *Walker River Chronology: A Chronological History of the Walker River and Related Water Issues.* Carson City, NV: Department of Conservation and Natural Resources, 1996.

Houghton, Samuel G. *A Trace of Desert Waters: The Great Basin Story.* 1976. Reprint, Reno: University of Nevada Press, 1994.

Hulse, James W. *The Silver State: Nevada's Heritage Reinterpreted*. Reno: University of Nevada Press, 2004.

Hunter, Joseph, Deputy Assistant Secretary of Water and Science, Department of Interior. Oral history interview by Glen Krutz. Washington, DC, May 21, 1991.

International Rivers. "Annual Reports, 2007." September 2008. http://www.internationalrivers.org/files/AnnualReport2007.pdf.

Jackson, W. Turrentine, and Donald J. Pisani. *A Case Study in Interstate Resource Management: The California-Nevada Water Controversy, 1865–1995*. Contribution no. 141. Davis: California Water Resources Center, May 1973.

———. *A Case Study in Interstate Resource Management: The California-Nevada Water Controversy, 1955–1968*. Contribution no. 147. Davis: California Water Resources Center, May 1974.

———. *Lake Tahoe Water: A Chronicle of Conflict Affecting the Environment*. Environmental Quality Series. Davis, CA: Institute of Governmental Affairs, 1972.

Jensen, Thomas C., Staff Attorney for the Senate Subcommittee on Water and Power. Oral history interview by Donald B. Seney. Washington, DC, November 11, 1995.

Johnson, Norma K., and Charles T. Dumar. "A Survey of Western Water Law in Response to Changing Economics and Public Interest Demands." *Natural Resources Journal* 29 (1989): 347–87.

Johnson, Troy R. "Roots of Contemporary Native American Activism." *American Indian Culture and Research Journal* (1996): 1–28.

Knack, Martha, and Omar C. Stewart. *As Long as the River Shall Run: A Ethnohistory of Pyramid Lake Indian Reservation*. Berkeley: University of California Press, 1989.

Laycock, George. "What Water for Stillwater?" *Audubon,* November 1988, 14–25.

MacDonnell, Laurence. "Federal Interests in Western Water Resources: Conflict and Accommodation." *Natural Resource Journal* 29 (1989): 389–411.

Mahin, Donald, Engineer, Washoe County Water Management Planning Division. Oral history interview by Richard Acton. Carson City, NV, October 4, 2001.

Martin, Russell. *A Story That Stands Like a Dam: Glen Canyon and the Struggle for the Soul of the West*. New York: Henry Holt, 1989.

McConnell, Lyman, Project Manager, Truckee Carson Irrigation District (TCID). Oral history interview by Donald B. Seney. Fallon, NV, August 19 and September 9, 1994.

McCool, Daniel C. *Command of the Waters: Iron Triangles, Federal Water Development, and Indian Water.* Berkeley: University of California Press, 1987.

———. *Command of the Waters: Iron Triangles, Federal Water Development, and Indian Water.* Berkeley: University of California Press, 1994.

———. "Indian Water Settlements: The Prerequisites of Successful Negotiation." *Policy Studies Journal* 21, no. 2 (1993): 227–43.

———. *Native Waters: Contemporary Indian Water Settlements and the Second Treaty Era.* Tucson: University of Arizona Press, 2002.

———. "Water Welfare and the New Politics of Water." *Halcyon* 14 (1992): 85–102.

McKinnon, Janet E. "Water to Waste: Irrational Decision-Making in the American West." *Harvard Environmental Law Review* 10, no. 2 (1986): 503–32.

Means, Russell, and Marvin J. Wolf. *Where White Men Fear to Tread: The Autobiography of Russell Means.* New York: St. Martin's Press, 1995.

Mehl, Wayne, Legislative Director, Office of Senator Harry Reid. Oral history interview by Glen Krutz. Washington, DC, May 20, 1991.

———. Oral history interview by Donald B. Seney. Washington, DC, November 7, 1995.

Moore, Michael R. "Native American Water Rights: Efficiency and Fairness." *Natural Resources Journal* 29 (1989): 761–91.

Morris, Edmund. *Theodore Rex.* New York: Random House, 2001.

Nagel, Joane. *American Indian Ethnic Renewal: Red Power and the Resurgence of Identity and Culture.* New York: Oxford University Press, 1996.

Nevada System of Higher Education. *Final Report, Phase One.* 2006. http://www.unr.edu/walker.

Oldam, Sue, Former Legal Counsel for Sierra Pacific Power Company. Interview by Leah J. Wilds. Reno, NV, March 18, 2008.

Olinger, Todd. *Trends and Directions in Federal Water Policy: A Summary of the Conference Proceedings, Report to the Western Water Policy Review Commission,* Phoenix, AZ. Springfield, VA: National Technical Information Service, 1997.

Overvold, David, Newlands Project Manager. Interview by Leah J. Wilds. Fallon, NV, July 24, 2008.

Pelcyger, Wayne, Pyramid Lake Tribal Attorney. Oral history interview by Glen Krutz. Reno, NV, March 6, 1991.

———. Oral history interview by Donald B. Seney. Reno, NV, September 27 and October 10, 1995.

Pisani, Donald J. *Water, Land, and Law in the West: The Limits of Public Policy, 1850–1920.* Lawrence: University Press of Kansas, 1996.

———. *Water and American Government: The Reclamation Bureau, National Water Policy, and the West, 1902–1935.* Berkeley: University of California Press, 2002.

Powell, John Wesley. *Exploration of the Colorado River and Its Canyons: A Report on the Lands of the Arid Region of the United States, with a More Detailed Account of the Lands of Utah.* Washington, DC: US Government Printing Office, 1876.

Reid, E. Leif. "Ripples from the Truckee: The Case for Congressional Apportionment of Disputed Interstate Water Rights." *Stanford Environmental Law Journal* 14 (1995): 145.

Reid, Senator Harry. Interview by Leah Wilds. Reno, NV, October 13, 2008.

———. "Statement of Harry Reid." Senate Subcommittee on Water and Power. Washington, DC: US Senate, April 12, 1994.

Reisner, Marc. *Cadillac Desert: The American West and Its Disappearing Water.* New York: Penguin Books, 1986.

Reisner, Marc, and Sarah Bates. *Overtapped Oasis: Reform or Revolution for Western Water?* Washington, DC: Island Press, 1990.

Rogers, Peter. *America's Water: Federal Roles and Responsibilities.* Cambridge: MIT Press, 1996.

Rowley, William D. *The Bureau of Reclamation: Origins and Growth to 1945.* Vol. 1. Denver: US Department of Interior, Bureau of Reclamation, 2006.

———. "The Newlands Project: Crime or National Commitment?" *Nevada Public Affairs Review* 2 (1992): 39–43.

———. *Reclaiming the Arid West: The Career of Francis G. Newlands.* Bloomington: Indiana University Press, 1996.

Rusco, Elmer, Emeritus Professor, Political Science, University of Nevada, Reno. Interview by Leah J. Wilds. Reno, NV, August 25, 2004.

———. "The Truckee-Carson–Pyramid Lake Water Rights Settlement Act and Pyramid Lake." *Nevada Public Affairs Review* 1 (1992): 9–14.

Sada, Don. Interview on *Preserving a Desert Treasure: Walker Basin Project* (DVD). Reno: University of Nevada, Reno, and the Desert Research Institute, 2009.

Sanford, Jim. Interview by Leah Wilds. Yerington, NV, March 25, 2008.

Scanland, Robert, Program Manager, Great Basin Land and Water. Interview by Leah J. Wilds. Reno, NV, February 28, 2008.

Seney, Donald B. "The Changing Political Fortunes of the Truckee-Carson Irrigation District." *Agricultural History* 76, no. 2 (2002): 220–31.

Shamberger, Hugh A. *Evolution of Nevada's Water Laws, as Related to the Development and Evaluation of the State's Water Resources, from 1866 to About 1960.* Nevada: USGS and Nevada Division of Water Resources, 1991.

Sharpe, Saxon E., Mary E. Cablk, and James M. Thomas. *The Walker Basin, Nevada and California: Physical Environment, Hydrology, and Biology.* Report 41231. Reno, NV: Desert Research Institute, 2007.

Simonds, William Joe. *The Newlands Project.* Denver: US Bureau of Reclamation, 1996.

Staller, N., Economist, Water Resources Branch, Office of Management and Budget. Oral history interview by Glen Krutz. Washington, DC, May 21, 1991.

Stalnaker, Clair, Leader, Aquatic Branch, National Ecology Research Center, US Fish and Wildlife Service, Department of the Interior. Telephone interviews by Leah J. Wilds, April 10, 1990, and April 15, 1991.

State Sovereignty as Impaired by Federal Ownership of Land. Carson City, NV: Legislative Counsel Bureau, 1982.

Stegner, Wallace. *Beyond the 100th Meridian: John Wesley Powell and the Second Opening of the West.* New York: Penguin Books, 1992.

Susskind, Laurence, and Jeffrey Cruikshank. *Breaking the Impasse: Consensual Approaches to Resolving Public Disputes.* New York: Basic Books, 1987.

Susskind, Laurence, and Connie Ozawa. "Mediated Negotiations in the Public Sector." *American Behavioral Scientist* 17, no. 2 (1983): 255–79.

Taylor, Tracy. *Nevada Water Facts.* Carson City, NV: Department of Conservation and Natural Resources, 2007.

Thorson, John E., Sarah Britton, and Bonnie G. Colby. *Tribal Water Rights: Essays in Contemporary Law, Policy, and Economics.* Tucson: University of Arizona Press, 2006.

Townley, John M. *Turn This Water into Gold: The Story of the Newlands Project.* Reno: Nevada Historical Society, 1998.

Tyler, Scott. Interview on *Preserving a Desert Treasure: Walker Basin Project* (DVD). Reno: University of Nevada, Reno, and the Desert Research Institute, 2009.

US Department of the Interior. *Executive Summary: Truckee River Operation*

Agreement, Final Environmental Impact Statement. Environmental Impact Report. Washington, DC: US Government Printing Office, 2008.

———. *Final Report of the Secretary of the Interior to the Congress of the United Sates of Newlands Project Efficiency Study.* Bureau of Reclamation. Washington, DC: US Government Printing Office, 1994.

US Senate. *Hearing Before the Subcommittee on Water and Power of the Committee on Energy and Natural Resources.* Washington, DC: US Government Printing Office, February 6, 1995.

US Senate, Select Committee on Indian Affairs. *Providing for the Settlement of Water Rights Claims of the Fallon Paiute Shoshone Indian Tribes.* Report 101-555. Washington, DC: US Government Printing Office, 1991.

Walker Basin Project. *Current Research, 2011–2013.* http://www.nevada /walker.

Walker Basin Research Projects. *Phase One, 2007–2009.* http://www.nevada /edu/walker.

Walker Basin Restoration Program. *Progress Report, 2010–2011.* http://www .nfwf.org.

Welden, Fred W. *History of Water Law in Nevada and the Western States.* Carson City, NV: Legislative Council Bureau, 2003.

WestWater Research. *Publication No. 04-11-011.* Pullman: Washington State University, Department of Ecology, July 2004.

Wheeler, Sessions S. *The Desert Lake: The Story of Nevada's Pyramid Lake.* Caldwell, ID: Caxton Press, 2001.

Wilds, Leah J. *Understanding Who Wins: Organizational Behavior and Environmental Politics.* New York: Garland Press, 1990.

———. *Water Politics in Northern Nevada: A Century of Struggle.* Reno: University of Nevada Press, 2010.

Wilds, Leah J., and Richard Acton. "Resolving the Water Dilemma: Past Problems and Future Trends." In *Towards 2000 Public Policy in Nevada,* edited by Dennis L. Soden and Eric Herzik. Dubuque, IA: Kendall/Hunt, 1997.

———. "The Saga Continues: Implementing the Negotiated Settlement." *Nevada Historical Society* 48, no. 2 (2005): 315–32.

Wilds, Leah J., Danny A. Gonzalez, and Glen A. Krutz. "Reclamation and the Politics of Change: The Truckee-Carson–Pyramid Lake Water Rights Settlement Act of 1990." *Nevada Historical Quarterly* 37, no. 3 (1994): 173–99.

Wondolleck, Julia M., and Steven L. Yaffe. *Making Collaboration Work: Lessons from Innovation in Natural Resource Management*. Washington, DC: Island Press, 2000.

Zell, Patricia, Democratic Staff Director and Chief Counsel, Senate Committee on Indian Affairs. Oral history interview by Glen Krutz. Washington, DC, May 21, 1991.

———. Oral history interview by Donald B. Seney. Washington, DC, March 27, 1997.

Index